ON DISNEY

EISEN

SERGEI

STEIN

ON
DISNEY

EDITED BY *Jay Leyda*
TRANSLATED BY *Alan Upchurch*
INTRODUCED BY *Naum Kleiman*

Seagull
BOOKS

LONDON NEW YORK CALCUTTA

SEAGULL BOOKS, 2017

First published by Seagull Books in 1986

English translation © Seagull Books, 1986

Introduction © Naum Kleiman

ISBN 978 0 85742 491 4

British Library Cataloguing-in-Publication Data
A catalogue record for this book is available from the British Library

Typeset by Manasij Dutta, Seagull Books, Calcutta, India
Printed and bound by Hyam Enterprises, Calcutta, India

CONTENTS

LIST OF ABBREVIATIONS

In the notes, Sergei Eisenstein is referred to as E and the following abbreviations are used for the commonly cited works:

ESW1: Sergei Eisenstein, *Selected Works, Volume 1: Writings, 1922–34* (Richard Taylor ed. and trans.). London: BFI, 1988.

ESW2: Sergei Eisenstein, *Selected Works, Volume 2: Towards a Theory of Montage* (Michael Glenny ed., R. Taylor trans.). London: BFI, 1991.

ESW3: Sergei Eisenstein, *Selected Works, Volume 3: Writings, 1934–47* (Richard Taylor ed., William Powell trans.). London: BFI, 1996.

ESW4: Sergei Eisenstein, *Beyond the Stars: The Memoirs of Sergei Eisenstein* (Richard Taylor ed., William Powell trans.). Calcutta: Seagull Books, 1995.

ER: Richard Taylor (ed.), *The Eisenstein Reader* (Richard Taylor and William Powell trans). London: BFI, 1998.

ERD: Ian Christie and Richard Taylor (eds), *Eisenstein Rediscovered*. London: Routledge, 1993.

FF: Richard Taylor and Ian Christie (eds), *The Film Factory: Russian and Soviet Cinema in Documents, 1896–1939* (Richard Taylor trans.). London: Routledge & Kegan Paul, 1988.

FEL: Sergei Eisenstein, *Film Essays and a Lecture* (Jay Leyda ed. and trans.). Princeton, NJ: Princeton University Press, 1982.

FiFo: Sergei Eisenstein, *Film Form: Essays in Film Theory*, (Jay Leyda ed. and trans.). New York: Harcourt, Brace Jovanovich, 1949.

FS: Sergei Eisenstein, *The Film Sense* (Jay Leyda ed. and trans.). New York: Harcourt, Brace Jovanovich, 1942.

IP: *Izbrannye proizvedeniia v shesti tomakh* [Selected Works in Six Volumes] (S. I. Iutkevich et al. eds). Moscow: Iskusstvo, 1964–71.

NIN: Sergei Eisenstein, *Nonindifferent Nature: Film and the Structure of Things* (Herbert Marshall ed. and trans.). Cambridge: Cambridge University Press, 1987.

RGALI: Rossiiskii gosudarstvennyi arkhiv literatury i iskusstv [Russian State Archive for Literature and the Arts], Moscow.

VGIK: Vsesoiuznyi gosudarstvennyi institut kinmetaografii [All-Union State Cinema Institute], Moscow.

INTRODUCTION

In approaching his article on Walt Disney, Eisenstein sought less to paint a literary portrait of the renowned animator (even though he knew him personally) or to trace his creative progress (even though he followed the studio's every new release). Disney's films became for Eisenstein merely the grounds for examining a single problem. But then, as he believed, these grounds were the most pressing, and the problem he considered central to the theory and practice of art in general. Eisenstein called it the

Grundproblem—the problem that was not only fundamental, but basic, underlying and foundational.

Briefly and simply, this problem may be defined as the
correlation of the rationally-logical and the sensuous in art:
in a creative act, in the structure of a work, in the process
of its perception. It first confronted Eisenstein at the dawn
of his own creative activity, when the young director set
himself the task of solving the mystery of the attractability
(attraktsionnost'—that is, the attractiveness and affective-
ness) of art. After a decade of experiments, discoveries and
crises, he arrived at the following conclusion:

> The dialectic of a work of art is constructed upon
> a most interesting 'dyad'. The effect of a work of
> art is built upon the fact that two processes are
> taking place within it simultaneously. There is a
> determined progressive ascent towards ideas at the
> highest peaks of consciousness and at the same
> time there is a penetration through the structure
> of form into the deepest layer of emotional
> thinking. The polarity between these two creates
> the remarkable tension of the unity of form and
> content that distinguishes genuine works. All gen-
> uine works possess it.[1]

This assertion formed the core of the conception of
the book, 'Method', on which Eisenstein worked for eight
years from 1940 to the final days of his life. As far as we

are able to tell at present, this unfinished book was to be made up of two large sections.

In the first section, the formation of the developing conception is reconstructed—the dramatic 'passage through purgatory' of the director-theoretician, who had discovered that the conceptual content of a work cannot be emotionally perceived by the viewer (reader, listener), if it does not simultaneously appeal to early ('pre-logical') forms of thought. The author of the theory of intellectual cinema, confused by this regressive tendency of art, undertakes excursuses into the fields of psychology, ethnography, linguistics, biology, aesthetics, philosophy. Both classical viewpoints, as well as the latest experiments, discoveries and hypotheses are subjected to thorough study. Eisenstein, by his own acknowledgement, draws for support on Lenin's 'Philosophical Notebooks':

> The history of philosophy, the history of the separate sciences, the history of the mental development of the child, the history of the mental development of animals, the history of language, N.B.: plus psychology, plus physiology of the sense organs—these are fields of knowledge from which the theory of knowledge and dialectics should be built.[2]

The Leninist definition of dialectics as the doctrine of the unity of opposition helps Eisenstein to overcome the tragic, inner 'rending of his soul': to reconcile the 'bi-directionality' of aesthetic experience in 'the highest unity of content and form'. By the end of the thirties, Eisenstein's Grundproblematik had found a sufficient theoretical conceptual framework.[3]

The second section of Eisenstein's Method was to consist of a series of sketches based upon the most wide-ranging material (from primitive plastics and Elizabethan tragedy to Degas and Picasso, from the drawings of Utamaro and the icons of Rublyov to the works of Rodin and Rilke), which would demonstrate the functioning of the laws he had substantiated.

Naturally, one of the central positions in this material was occupied by cinema—and not only in examples from Eisenstein's own films. Also in 1940, when Eisenstein was starting to expound the Grundproblematik, he began three articles on the outstanding masters of cinema, the influence of whose art had been truly proven by the worldwide recognition of viewers. Their names—D. W. Griffith, Charlie Chaplin and Walt Disney.

The discoveries by the patriarch of the art of film, Griffith, in the realm of montage and close-up (and the achievements of literature and painting preceding them) made it possible to show in action one of the mechanisms of early forms of thought—pars pro toto ('a part in place of the whole'), the basis of metonymy and metaphor in poetics. To this problem was devoted the investigation, 'The History of the Close-up Through the History of Art', a published fragment of which became widely known under the title *Dickens, Griffith and the Film Today*.[4]

The central theme of the article on Chaplin—'Charlie the Kid'[5]—became the 'infantilism' of the great comedian: those traits of the child's view of the world which conditioned also the imagery of his films, and the behaviour on the screen of his characters.

Finally, Disney provided direct grounds and material for an analysis of the survival of animism and totemism in modern consciousness and art: the very principle of the type of cinema in which Disney worked (and which unfortunately received in Russian the purely technical name, multiplikatsiia) consisted in the animation not only of animals and plants, but of the entire objective world.

But the matter, as customary for Eisenstein, was not restricted to a substantiation of the chosen thesis. Disney's type of animation—the continuous transformation of the animated contour line—led Sergei Mikhailovich, who also, incidentally, drew with an enclosing mathematical line, to the theme of protoplasmaticness, which lowered the level of attractiveness to the verge of 'the physiology of the sense organs'. In Eisenstein's view, the very mechanism of a flowing omnipotent contour was an echo of the most concealed depths of pre-memory. (We should note in parentheses that the idea of 'intracellular' memory, while sounding quite exotic in the 1940s, appears not at all heretical in light of the latest discoveries in genetics and cytology.) Disney's works recalled another problem that occupied Eisenstein—the 'synchronization of the senses' in sound film: in particular, the co-ordination of music and image, moving in space and time. This theme—from the phenomenon of synaesthesia to audio-visual counterpoint (in *Alexander Nevsky*)—was examined in another investigation of 1940, 'Vertical Montage'[6] and later, many pages of 'Nonindifferent Nature and Colour' were devoted to it.[7]

As was often the case with Eisenstein, the growing bulk of material prevented the completion of the article. The manuscripts from various years remained unpolished by the author into an integral, definitive text.

The earliest fragments of *On Disney* were written in September and October 1940. In our publication, however, they have comprised the second section, as the introductory pages to the article appeared a year later, in

Alma-Ata, where the Mosfilm studio had been evacuated after the German invasion. The other notes, dated November 1941, constitute the third section. Having returned at that time to the article, Eisenstein outlined anew the plan of the investigation, accenting several new aspects of the problems already expounded, and he then returned to the initial theme of totemism and animism. Apparently, the preparations begun shortly thereafter for the shooting of Ivan the Terrible, and the work on a new version of Method, interrupted work on *On Disney*. But the article was not abandoned for good. Over the course of the following years, Eisenstein returned time and again to Disney in numerous extracts, observations and journal notes. The most essential of these texts are presented in the fourth section.

In preparing the materials of the article for publication, we have not tried to give them the appearance of a fully completed text. On the contrary, we have preserved their fragmentariness, emphasized by indications of the dates of writing, and the multilingualisms, characteristic of Eisenstein's first draft manuscripts. The article's original manuscripts are preserved in the Central State Archive of Literature and Art of the USSR (TsGALI).[8] In the commentary, books with marginal notes by the director have been used from the library of the S. M. Eisenstein

Scientific-Memorial Cabinet under the Association of
Film-makers of the USSR.

Naum Kleiman, Curator
S. M. Eisenstein Scientific–Memorial Cabinet
Moscow [1986]

NOTES

1 From E's address to the All Union Creative Conference of Soviet Filmworkers on 8 January 1935, *ESW3*, pp. 16–41. This extract is from p. 38. Cf. 'Film Form: New Problems' in *FiFo*, pp. 144–5.

2 V. I. Lenin, 'Philosophical Notebooks' in *Collected Works*, VOL. 38 (C. Dutt trans.) (Moscow: Foreign Languages Publishing House, 1961), pp. 352–3.

3 A number of the materials and positions of the cited circle of investigations have been illuminated and commented upon by V.V. Ivanov in his book, Ocherki po istorii semiotiki v SSSR [Essays on the History of Semiotics in the USSR], Moscow: Nauka, 1979. An English translation of some of Ivanov's writings appears in 'Film Theory and General Semiotics', Russian *Poetics in Translation*, VOL. 8 (Oxford: RPT, 1981).

4 *FiFo*, pp. 122–49.

5 *ESW3*, pp. 243–67; *FEL*, pp. 108–39.

6 *ESW2*, pp. 327–99; FS, pp. 60–91 and 123–68.

7 These two unfinished books were both first published in Russian in: *IP3*. *Colour* still awaits a full English translation.

8 Now the Central State Archive of Literature and Art of the Russian Federation (RGALI).

ON
DISNEY

Eisenstein and Disney at the Disney Studio, 1930.
(Eisenstein Cabinet)

I

[*Alma-Ata, 16, November 1941*]

Begin with:

'The work of this master is the greatest contribution of the American people to art.'

Dozens and dozens of newspaper clippings, modifying this sentence in various ways, pour down upon the astonished master. They are all from different statements, in different places, to different newspapers and different journalists. And they all come from one and the same man. A Russian film-maker who had just landed upon the North American continent. However, the same news had already preceded him from England. There, for the first time and on the very first day of his arrival on British soil, he had rushed off to see the works of the man upon whom he had showered such passionate praise in all his interviews. Thus, long before their meeting in person, friendly relations had been established between praiser and praised. Between a Russian and an American. In short, between Disney and myself. When we met each other in person, we met like old acquaintances. And all the more so since he also knew our pictures.

Young and with a small moustache. Very elegant. The elegance of a dancer, I'd say. There's undeniably something of his own hero in him. Mickey has the same grace, ease of gesture and elegance. Not at all surprising!

As later becomes clear, his method is as follows: Disney himself acts out the part or role of Mickey for this or that film. A dozen or so artists stand around him in a circle, quickly capturing the hilarious expressions of their posing and performing boss. And the extremely lively and lifelike preparations for the cartoon are ready—infectious through the whole hyperbolization of the drawing only because it was taken from a living person. No less alive are the Wolf, the Bear, the Hound (the coarse partner of the refined Mickey); again not accidentally full of life, he comes from Walt's first cousin who, in contrast to him, is chubby, coarse and clumsy.

We tour his tiny studio, far, far away in those days from the centre of Hollywood vanity and life. We are amazed by the modesty of his equipment, considering the colossal scale of productivity. 52 'Mickeys' a year,[1] plus twelve *Silly Symphonies*, including the unsurpassed *The Skeleton Dance*,[2] with the skeletons who play on their own ribs as xylophones! We are surprised by the harmony of the collective. By the harmony of technique. And especially by the fact that the soundtrack is made in New York, where they send the most precisely marked rolls of the drawings' movements, shot to the most precise music score. Not in the slightest resulting in Impressionism. Disney's plastic visions, echoing the sounds, are captured a priori. Placed in a vise of the strictest plastic and temporal calculation. Made real. Coordinated by the dozens of hands of his collective. Shot on irreproachable rolls carrying charm, laughter and amazement at his virtuosity around the entire world.

••

I am sometimes frightened when I watch his films. Frightened because of some absolute perfection in what he does. This man seems to know not only the magic of every technical means, but also all the most secret strands of human thought, images, ideas, feelings. Such was probably the effect of St Francis of Assisi's sermons. Fra Angelico's paintings bewitch in this way.[3] He creates somewhere in the realm of the very purest and most primal depths. There, where we all are children of nature. He creates on the conceptual level of man not yet shackled by logic, reason, or experience. That is how butterflies fly. That is how flowers grow. That is how brooks marvel at their own course. That is how Andersen and Alice charm in Wonderland.[4] That is how Hoffman wrote in lighter moments.[5] The same current of interflowing images. The archivist Lindhorst,[6] who is also King of the Elves, etc. One of Disney's most amazing films is his *Merbabies*.[7] What purity and clarity of soul is needed to make such a thing! To what depths of untouched nature is it necessary to dive with bubbles and bubble-like children in order to reach such absolute freedom from all categories, all conventions. In order to be like children.

The very last line written by Gogol's hand was: 'For only as a child may you enter the Holy Kingdom.'

Chaplin, too, is infantile. But his is a constant, agonized and, somewhere at its core, an always tragic lament over the lost golden age of childhood. The epos of Chaplin is the 'Paradise Lost' of today. The epos of Disney is 'Paradise Regained'. Precisely Paradise. Unreachable on Earth. Created only by a drawing. It is not the absurdity of childish conceptions of an eccentric clashing with adult reality. The humour of the incompatibility of one with the other. And the sadness over man's forever-lost childhood, and mankind's Golden Age, lost irretrievably to those who want to bring it back from the past, instead of creating it in a better Socialist future. Disney (and it is no accident that his films are drawn) is a complete return to a world of complete freedom (not accidentally fictitious), freed from the necessity of another primal extinction.

• •

As an unforgettable symbol of his whole creative work, there stands before me a family of octopuses on four legs, with a fifth serving as a tail, and a sixth—a trunk. How much (imaginary) divine omnipotence there is in this! What magic of reconstructing the world according to one's fantasy and will! A fictitious world. A world of lines and colours which subjugates and alters itself to your command. You tell a mountain: move, and it moves. You tell an octopus: be an elephant, and the octopus becomes an elephant. You ask the sun to stop, and it stops.

You are able to see how the image of the hero who stopped the sun arose among those who were powerless to even take cover from it, and whose whole way of life was at the mercy of the sun. And you see how the drawn magic of a reconstructed world had to arise at the very summit of a society that had completely enslaved nature—namely, in America. Where, at the same time, man has become more merciless than in the Stone Age, more doomed than in prehistoric times, more enslaved than during the slave-owning era.[8]

Disney is a marvellous lullaby for the suffering and unfortunate, the oppressed and deprived. For those who are shackled by hours of work and regulated moments of rest, by a mathematical precision of time, whose lives are graphed by the cent and dollar. Whose lives are divided up into little squares, like a chess board, with the sole difference that whether you're a knight or a rook, a queen or a bishop—on this board, you can only lose. And also because its black squares do not alternate with white ones, but are all of a protective grey colour, day after day. Grey, grey, grey. From birth to death. Grey squares of city blocks. Grey prison cells of city streets. Grey faces of endless street crowds. The grey, empty eyes of those who are forever at the mercy of a pitiless procession of laws, not of their own making, laws that divide up the soul, feelings, thoughts, just as the carcasses of pigs are dismembered by the conveyor belts of Chicago slaughterhouses, and the separate pieces of cars are assembled into mechanical organisms by Ford's conveyor belts. That is why Disney's films blaze with colour. Like the patterns in the clothes of people who have been deprived of the colours in nature. That is why the imagination in them is limitless, for Disney's films are a revolt against partitioning and legislating, against spiritual stagnation and greyness. But the revolt is lyrical. The revolt is a daydream. Fruitless and lacking consequences. These are not those daydreams which, accumulating, give birth to action and raise a hand to realize the dream. They are the golden dreams you escape to, like other worlds where everything is different, where you are free from all fetters, where you can clown around just as nature itself seemed to have done in the joyful ages of its coming into being, when she herself invented curiosities worthy of Disney: the ridiculous ostrich next to the logical hen, the absurd giraffe next to the loyal cat, the kangaroo mocking the future Madonna!

Disney's beasts, fish and birds have the habit of stretching and shrinking. Of mocking at their own form, just as the fish-tiger and octopus-elephant of *Merbabies* mock at the categories of zoology. This triumph over the fetters of form is symptomatic. This triumph over all fetters, over everything that binds, resounds throughout, from the plastic trick to the hymn of *The Three Little Pigs*: 'We're not afraid of the big, grey wolf . . .'⁹

With that triumphant joy, the millions of hearts join in this chorus, who every moment are afraid of the big grey wolf. The 'grey wolf' in America is behind every corner, behind every counter, on the heels of every person. One moment, he blows away to the auction block which is the home and property of a farmer ruined by the financial crisis, another moment, he blows out of his comfortable house a man who has worked many years for Ford, but who could not make his last payment. Frightening, frightening is the 'grey wolf' of unemployment: millions and millions of people are gobbled up by its voracious appetite.

But 'we're not afraid of the big, grey wolf' flies carefree from the screen. This cry of optimism could only be drawn. For there is no such slant on truthfully shot capitalist reality which, without lying, could possibly sound like optimistic reassurance, but, fortunately, there are lines and colours. Music and cartoons. The talent of Disney and the 'great consoler'—the cinema.

∙∙

There exists a touching legend from the Middle Ages about 'The Juggler of the Holy Mother'. A pilgrimage was made to bring gifts to the Madonna. He alone had nothing to take her. And so he spread out his mat before her statue and honoured her with his art. This did not please the fat monks and greedy priest: they preferred fat and candles, silver coins and wine. But, even so, the legend of the juggler was preserved with reverence, even by them.

This is how Americans, once they start to undertake the realization of the Golden Age of the future, will recall with warmth and gratitude the man who cheered them up with golden dreams during their period of oppression.

Who, for an instant, allowed them to forget, to not feel the chilling horror before the grey wolf who, while you were at the movies, pitilessly turned off your gas and water for non-payment. Who gave a feeling of warmth and closeness with grasshoppers and birds, beasts and flowers to those whose dungeons of the streets of New York were always cut off from everything happy and alive.[10]

17 November 1941

Among the strange characteristics of the tribes who populate this continent, North America, is the one by which its inhabitants choose specific stars for themselves and live their lives in worship of them.

These are not stars of heaven, but of the movies, but that does not change matters. It even provides a way of strengthening the financial resources of the Postal Service through an unending flood of letters addressed to beloved stars.

The American magazine, *The New Yorker*, once ran a cartoon making fun of this strangeness and passion of its fellow tribesmen. An elderly lady from the very highest society, with a diamond diadem in her grey hair and a discreet butler bowing in the background, is busy at the same activity as any young shop girl or office boy: she is writing to her favourite star . . .

But the point is not in the act of writing itself.

The point is the addressee.

The letter begins with the greeting: 'Dear Mickey Mouse'.

That is the point.

The huge, all-embracing, international popularity among all ages which is possessed by this small, drawn hero of the great artist and master, Walt Disney, who exceeds in popularity that other American by the name of Walt—Walt Whitman.[11]

Truly, all ages—from children to the elderly, all nationalities, all races and all types of social systems are intoxicated by him with the same delight, surrender with the same fervour to his charm, with the same ecstasy allow themselves to be carried away by Disney's living drawings (animated cartoons).

How is this achieved?

First of all, one could say that Disney's works seem to contain all the faultlessly active features by which a work of art influences—seemingly in the greatest possible quantity and the greatest possible purity.

In terms of the faultlessness of its influence, Disney's work statistically scores the greatest possible number of points, considering the viewers won over by it.

And our supposition, therefore, is entirely legitimate.

We shall try to enumerate the peculiarities and characteristic, features which distinguish Disney's work. And we shall try to generalize these features. They shall prove to be decisive features in any art form, but only in Disney, presented in their very purest form.

II

[*Kratovo*],[12] *21 September 1940*

Childhood recollections have deposited three scenes in my memory.

The first was from a reader. Some poem about an Arab in the desert and his crazed camel. About a mad camel who chases his master. About how the Arab, fleeing from the camel, falls into a precipice, but catches hold of a bush hanging over the bottomless abyss.

And about how, in the middle of this hopeless situation —with the infuriated camel above him and the bottomless precipice below—the Arab suddenly notices two or three red berries on the bush and, forgetting about everything, reaches for them.

The next recollection is vaguer, it must be earlier. In it, some sort of odd, sentimental angels are allowed to descend into Hell to lay their refreshing hands for an instant upon the heads of sinners boiling in pitch. Or, perhaps, to let a drop of moisture fall upon their thirst-tortured lips.

The third recollection is more concrete. It has an author—Victor Hugo, a precise place of action—Paris, and specific names of characters. His name is Quasimodo. Hers is Esmeralda. Accompanied by an elegant little goat, Esmeralda goes up to Quasimodo, who has been cruelly whipped and chained to a scaffold; to Quasimodo, suffering and tormented by thirst and the crowd's mockery. She lets him drink and gently presses her lips against his hideous, tortured, suffering face.

While watching Disney's *Snow White*,[13] I recall these three scenes.

But not because Snow White kisses the funny and ugly gnomes one by one on their bald heads; not because a flock of no less elegant deer and wild goats follows behind her; and not because she is surrounded by fairy tale terrors and horrors.

But because Disney's works themselves strike me as the same kind of drop of comfort, an instant of relief, a fleeting touch of lips in the hell of social burdens, injustices and torments, in which the circle of his American viewers is forever trapped.

Beyond the framework of the poem, the Arab, of course, will fall into the precipice or will be trampled to death by the camel. The sinners will go on suffering in the cauldrons of boiling pitch. The angels' caress, the two or three refreshing berries. Esmeralda's cup and goat will in no way change their fate. But for an instant, for a fraction of a second, they give them the most precious thing in their situation—obliviousness.

And Disney, like all of them, through the magic of his works—and more intensely perhaps than anyone else—bestows precisely this upon his viewer, precisely obliviousness, an instant of complete and total release from everything connected with the suffering caused by the social conditions of the social order of the largest capitalist government.

Disney neither brands, nor exposes.

We are used to the beasts in fables. The beasts there provide no comfort.

They do not bite the reader, do not scratch, do not growl at him and do not kick.

But they do something a lot less pleasant: they hold a distorting mirror up to their bigger brother—man.

This is how he thinks, the bigger brother, man. His own . . . snout is actually warped.

And this disturbing exposure is further aided by his smaller brothers—goats and sheep, foxes and lions, eagles and snakes, frogs and monkeys.

Disney's [beasts] do not expose anyone, do not blame and do not preach.

And if most of them did not flash by us so quickly in one or two short little reels, we could be made angry by the moral uselessness of their existence on the screen.

But because of the fleeting ephemerality of their existence, you cannot reproach them for their mindlessness.

Even the string of a bow cannot be strained for ever.

The same for the nerves.

And instants of this releasing—an expression which unsuccessfully conveys the sense of the word, relax, untranslatable [into Russian] —are just as prophylactically necessary as the daily dose of carefree laughter in the well-known American saying: 'A laugh a day keeps the doctor away.'

The triumphant proletariat of a future America will erect no monument to Disney as a fighter either in their hearts, or on street squares.

Memory will not crown his brow with the glory of a fabulist or a lampoonist, if you can even call a 'brow' the merry, moustachiod, mocking and ironically affable face of the creator of Mickey Mouse.

But everyone will recall him with warm gratitude for those instants of respite amid the torrential, desperate struggle for life and existence which he gave to the viewer in the troubled years of the social paradise of democratic America.

..

We know many workers in cinema who also lead the viewer to an obliviousness of the truth of life and to the golden dreams of a lie.

We know the concealed purpose of this. We have seen the fluffy dramatizations of similar spectacles off the screen as well.

With the same goal—to distract the attention of the man on the street from the genuine and serious problems of the interrelation of labour and capital to such absurd pseudo-problems as the struggle around the 'Dry Law'.[14]

And here too, as in the corresponding works, obliviousness is evil.

Obliviousness as a means of lulling to sleep; obliviousness as a way of distracting thought from the real to the fantastic; obliviousness as a tool for disarming the struggle.

This is not what Disney gives us.

In contrast to the big American screen, the small screen of Disney's cartoons does not deliver a pile of happy ends—happy only on the screen; nor a gilded lie about the fast-paced, honest careers and generosity of capitalist magnates; nor a base sermon, slurring over social contradictions. Without encouraging us to fight against this evil, neither does he naturally serve the cause of this evil by hiding behind a hypocritical: 'I'm not responsible for what I create'.

Disney is simply 'beyond good and evil'. Like the sun, like trees, like birds, like the ducks and mice, deer and pigeons that run across his screen. To an even greater degree than Chaplin. Than Chaplin, who sermonizes and often gets lost in Quakerizing.

Disney's films, while not exposing sunspots, themselves act like reflections of sunrays and spots across the screen of the earth.

They flash by, burn briefly and are gone.

In a certain French song, a cat stole a round piece of cheese, but the obliging moon placed on the empty dish a little white round reflection of the lunar disc.

He who takes it into his head to bite hold of Disney by the usual analysis and yardstick, the ordinary requirements, the standard norms, inquiries and demands of high genres of art—will gnash his teeth at the empty air. And still, this is a joyful and beautiful art that sparkles with a refinement of form and dazzling purity.

As much a paradox in the community of the serious arts, as the unprincipled but eternal circus, as the singing of a bird—lacking any content, but infinitely exciting in its warbling.

And, perhaps, precisely in this lies the especially curious nature of the method and means of Disney's art, as the purest model of *inviolably natural* elements, characteristic of any art and here presented in a chemically pure form.

Here it is like an aroma produced without a flower; a taste extracted from a fruit; sound as such; affect freed from any purpose.

How is this amazing phenomenon achieved?

To a certain extent, of course, it only seems to be so.

For at the centre of Disney, as well, stands man. But man brought back, as it were, to those pre-stages that were traced out by . . . Darwin.

In *Merbabies*, a striped fish in a cage is transformed into a tiger and roars with the voice of a lion or panther. Octopuses turn into elephants. A fish—into a donkey. A

quite dull and stupid for things to
go on in the common way
    So she set to work, and very
soon finished off the cake

* * * * *

    "Curiouser and curiouser!" cried
Alice, (she was so surprised that she
quite forgot how to speak good English,)
"now I'm opening out like the largest
telescope that ever was! Goodbye,
feet!" (for when she looked down
at her feet, they seemed almost
out of sight, they were getting so
far off) "oh, my poor little feet, I
wonder who will put on your shoes
and stockings for you now, dears?
I'm sure I can't! I shall be a great
deal too far off to bother myself about
you : you must manage the best
way you can — but I must be kind
to them", thought Alice, "or perhaps
they won't walk the way I want
to go! Let me see : I'll give them
a new pair of boots every Christmas".
    And she went on planning
to herself how she would manage it.

11

Facsimile of Lewis Carroll's manuscript of
Alice's Adventures Underground (1864).

John Tenniel's version of Alice (1865).

Walter Trier, cover illustration to Erich Kästner's *Arthur mit demlangen Arm* (1931) (Butler Library, Columbia University).

TOP: 'An Attractive Beauty'. Woodcut by Toyohiro (1828).
BOTTOM: 'Rewarded Gallantry'. Woodcut by Bokusen (early 19th century).

Print by Katsushika Hokusai.

departure from one's self. From once and forever prescribed norms of nomenclature, form and behaviour. Here it is overt. In the open. And, of course, in comic form. Seriously, as in life—and especially in American life—there is no such thing, it does not occur and cannot.

Is this a motif in Disney's works, or chance?

Let us look at some other films.

Let us examine the characteristics of the pre-colour Mickey Mouses.

What do you remember from them? A lot. There is the steamboat that folds logs like pastries; there are the hotdogs whose skins are pulled down and are spanked; there are the piano keys which bite the pianist like teeth, and much, much more.

And here too, of course, are the same traits of a transformed world, a world going out of itself. The world around the author—an inhuman world, and probably for that very reason inciting Disney to humanize Wilbur the grasshopper, Goofy the dog, Donald Duck, and first and foremost, Mickey and Minnie.

But one external trait especially sticks in the mind—a purely formal one, it would seem.

Mickey starts to sing, his hands folded together. The hands echo the music as only the movements of Disney's characters are capable of echoing a melody. And then reaching for a high note, the arms shoot up far beyond the limits of their normal representation. In tone to the music, they stretch far beyond the length allotted them. The necks of his surprised horses stretch the same way, or their legs become extended when running.

This is repeated by the necks of ostriches, the tails of cows, not to mention al the attributes of the beasts and plants in the *Silly Symphonies*, shot so as to meticulously coil to the tone and melody of the music.

And here too, as we see, there seems to be the same playing at something else, 'the impossible'.

But here it is deeper and broader.

In this aspect, is it characteristic only of Disney?

To solve the secret meaning of this phenomenon, let us look for examples beyond Disney's works.

Disney has become on the screen what *Alice in Wonderland* by Lewis Carroll was in the 1870s in the world of books.

The same rabbits with vest pockets, rats and mice, turtles and walruses live in its pages.

And, in the very first two chapters of her adventures, we find what we are looking for.

Alice is in a desperate situation: in Carroll's method, this is presented literally—there are no ways out from the place she had landed in, having fallen through a rabbit hole.

That is, there are some doors, but they are all locked.

And moreover, the doors are so small that at best, her head could get through, but certainly not her shoulders. 'Drink me' is written on a little bottle on a little table next to a little golden key to the door.

'" . . . what a curious feeling!" said Alice. "I must be shutting up like a telescope."

[She had drunk the contents of the little bottle.]

. . . And so it was indeed: she was now only ten inches high, and her face brightened up at the thought that she was now the right size for going through the little door into that lovely garden. First, however, she waited for a few minutes to see if she was going to shrink any further: she felt a little nervous about this; "for it might end, you know," said Alice to herself, "in my going out altogether, like a candle. I wonder what I should be like then?" And she tried to fancy what the flame of a candle looks like after the candle is blown out, for she could not remember ever having seen such a thing.'

But Alice does not manage to go out into the garden. She forgot the little key to the door on the table, and now her small height prevents her from reaching it. And her attempts to scramble onto the table along its leg are useless —it proves to be too slippery.

Alice starts to cry.

'Eat me'—is the beautiful writing on a little cake.

'Curiouser and curiouser!'—cries Alice who ate it:

'"Now I'm opening out like the largest telescope that ever was! Goodbye, feet!" (for when she looked down at her feet, they seemed to be almost out of sight, they were getting so far off). "Oh, my poor little feet, I wonder who will put on your shoes and stockings for you now, dears? I'm sure *I* shan't be able! I shall be a great deal too far off to trouble myself about you ..."'

Alice is now so huge that again she cannot pass through the doors of the underground room.

In a new fit of despair, she starts to shed tears, but suddenly she notices that she has quickly started to shrink again: the reason for this is the fan that she has been waving back and forth. She just barely manages to throw it away before she disappears completely, and then suddenly falls into a lake of tears—her own tears she had shed when she was huge. "I wish I hadn't cried so much!" says Alice, swimming about the salty waves. But we'll leave her here, for the episode of expanding and shrinking height which interests us is over.[15]

Wilhelm Busch, *Max and Moritz* (1865).

Is there a borrowing here by Disney? Or is this image of elasticity of shapes generally widespread?

I find it in the drawings of the German caricaturist, Trier.[16] The adventures of a little boy with a very long arm.

But this same image I also find among 18th-century Japanese etchings. The many-metred arms of geishas reaching out after frightened customers through the gratings of the Yoshiwara teahouses.[17]

More ancient are patterns with an abstract interplay of infinitely stretching necks, legs and noses. Stretched noses are the property of even an entire breed of mythological beings—the Tengu, etc. Moreover, I recall the circus arenas and the entirely incomprehensible interest which has compelled hundreds of thousands of people over the centuries to follow with bated breath this same thing which the stage and variety artist is capable of doing within the limits of human possibilities: before the viewer is a 'human snake'—a spineless, elastic creature, for some reason most often dressed as Mephistopheles, if it's not by chance the 'Snake Dancer' of New York's Negro nightclubs, where the same kind of creature writhes in abstract, silk robes . . .

The attractiveness of this process is obvious. I purposely cited it as the first example in the very purest and even abstract and story-less form. This does not mean that it cannot be used as a working model for loftier, moralizing and philosophical purposes. And without losing any of its 'attractionness', as I called a similar attraction in my youth, which imparts a warm lifelikeness and vital imagery to the most morally-ethical thesis. For are not there echoes of the attractiveness of this very phenomenon in the fate of the shrinking skin which serves as the central image of Balzac's *La Peau de chagrin*?[18] An image which is profound in thought and irresistibly attractive and exciting in form?

What is strange is not the fact that it exists.

What is strange is that it attracts.

And you cannot help but arrive at the conclusion that a single, common prerequisite of attractiveness shows through in all these examples: a rejection of once-and-forever allotted form, freedom from ossification, the ability to assume dynamically any form.

An ability that I would call 'plasmaticness', for here we have a being represented in drawing, a being of a definite form, a being which has attained a definite appearance, and which behaves like the primal protoplasm, not yet possessing a stable form, but capable of assuming any form and which, skipping along the rungs of the evolutionary ladder, attaches itself to any and all forms of animal existence.

Why is the sight of this so attractive?

It is difficult to assume in the viewer a memory of his own existence at a similar stage—the origin of the foetus or further back down the evolutionary scale (even if one measures the depth of the base of memory not just as it resides in the brain, but in all its predecessors, right down to the cellular tissue).

But it is easier to accept that this picture is inescapably attractive through its trait of all-possible diversity of form. In a country and social order with such a mercilessly standardized and mechanically measured existence, which is difficult to call life, the sight of such omnipotence (that is, the ability to become 'whatever you wish'), cannot but hold a sharp degree of attractiveness. This is as true for the United States as it is for the petrified canons of world-outlook, art and philosophy of eighteenth century Japan. This is also true for the starch-bound and tuxedoed habitué of nightclubs who feasts his eyes upon the boneless elastic figures, who know nothing of the rigid spine and stiff corset of high society.

A lost changeability, fluidity, suddenness of formations—that is the subtext brought to the viewer who lacks all this by these seemingly strange traits which permeate folktales, cartoons, the spineless circus performer and the seemingly groundless scattering of extremities in Disney's drawings.[19]

[It is natural to expect that such a strong tendency of the transformation of stable forms into forms of mobility could not be confined solely to means of form: this tendency exceeds the boundaries of form and extends to subject and theme. An unstable character becomes a film hero; that is, the kind of character for whom a changeable appearance is natural. Here, changeability of form is no longer a paradoxical expressiveness, as in the case of stretching necks, tails and legs: here, God Himself commanded the character to be fluid.

Such a picture is about ghosts. Here, Mickey and his friends are members of a company that exterminates ghosts.[20] And the whole film draws peripeteias of a heated hunt for ghosts throughout a deserted house. There is no limit here to the outburst of transformations of a greenish cloud with the appearance of red-nosed mischievous ghosts. But the film is further remarkable in that the basic theme here appears distinctly in the whole solution of the thing.

This film, if you will, is not only nostalgia and daydreaming about the liberation of forms from the laws of logic and forever established stability, as it was in *Merbabies*. This film, if you will, is a challenge, and its 'moral'—an appeal to the fact that, only having loosened the fetters of stability is the attainment of life possible. Indeed, we will look upon this opus not as a work rolling gaily along beside us, but as a document that has come down to us, of certain eras and tendencies, like folk tales of antiquity or myths. And its tendencies will become completely clear. The *Ghost Exterminating Company*—is this not actually a symbol of formal logic which drives out everything living, mobile, fantastical? Its failures and losses in the war with a handful of ghosts, with the fantastic which lurks I the nature of every night table, in every soup bowl, behind every door and in every wall! And the victory over ghosts? It is provided by a charming scene: the frightened 'agents' of the war with ghosts, after a thousand and one adventures where they are duped by the ghosts, fall into a mass of dough. Just like Max and Moritz.[21] Here, however, they do not become gingerbread men, but run around as terrifying white shadows, dragging their tails of dough. Their appearance is fantastic, ghostly. They themselves become like ghosts. And then what? The ghosts themselves, frightened by them, take off like a bullet from the 'haunted' house! A stroke of pure Disney charm. In essence—a unique morality play on the theme that, only having joined in the fantastical, alogical and sensuous order is it possible to achieve a mastery and supremacy in the realm of freedom from the shackles of logic, from shackles in general.

This is a fictitious freedom. For an instant. A momentary, imaginary, comical liberation from the time-lock mechanism of American life. A five-minute 'break' for the psyche, but during which the viewer himself remains chained to the winch of the machine.[22]

But at the same time, this situation is also a symbol of Disney's method. For through his whole system of devices, themes and subjects, Disney constantly gives us prescriptions for folkloric, mythological, pre logical thought—but always rejecting, pushing aside logic, brushing aside logistics, formal logic, the logical case.

Let us take another example. Who else is in a silly situation in a film about prescriptions for self-control?[23] Who masters himself, who instead of giving free reign to his impulses, obediently repeats the prescription broadcast on the radio, and meekly counts off 1, 2, 3 ... up to 10?

And with what delight Donald Duck smashes this machine of self-discipline and self-control—the radio, after having suffered over the course of the picture a thousand and one misfortunes, in which he had inhibited his own spontaneity and consciously tried to fetter and enslave it to please the hypocritically sanctimonious voice from the radio, which appealed to the purely Christian virtue of the enslavement of one's own individuality. In what a flood of treacle flows the same kind of sermon throughout the United States—the innumerable churches, brotherhoods, sermons, leaflets, societies! How powerful in America is this Christmas-time appeal of the Salvation Army and the followers of Mary Baker Eddy ('Christian Science') and Aimee McPherson:[24] to make the shackles imposed by the social order on the life and existence of its free people glow as virtues.

Disney does not go into the roots. But has fun and entertains, mocks and amuses—jumping like a squirrel from branch to branch somewhere along the very surface of the phenomenon, without looking beneath to the origins, at the reasons and causes, at the conditions and pre-conditions.

But the unstable hero with purely protean greed seeks ever newer and newer forms of embodiment.

Mobility of contour is not enough for him. The play of waters, moving like a giant, living, formless amoeba in *Hawaiian Holiday*[25] with Goofy and his surfboard, are not enough for him. (In one of his black-and-white films, the waves, thus playing, tousle a steamship, gathering into puffs of foam, puffs which suddenly become fists in boxing gloves, delivering punches to the poor sides of the steamships.) The collapsible steamship which arises from a system of bolls to scatter suddenly again into nothing, is not enough for him. (Elastic necks of contours are stretched here to the gigantic proportions of a whole ship arising from nothing again dissolving into nothing.) The interplay of storm clouds in the sky and the greenish cloud of endlessly changing ghosts inside the deserted house, is not enough for him. The ghostly mask which prophesies to the witch in *Snow White*, appears in fire. And what, if not fire, is capable of most fully conveying the dream of a flowing diversity of forms?

And thus arises *The Moth and the Flame*.[26]]

Its hero is—fire.

There exist many explanations for the mysterious attractiveness of fire.

Including some deeply suppressed sexual interpretations by German sexologists, compelling German criminologists to attribute 'aimless' arsons to the category of crimes of a sexual nature. Thus, the well-known criminologist, Dr Erich Wulffen, allots an entire chapter to this question in his book, *Der Sexualverbrecher*.[27]

More interesting and convincing is the incidental material which he touches upon indirectly in connection with these questions.

Here he cites Bloch's[28] opinion on how, besides the survival of the common infantile institution of destruction (for example, in the breaking and smashing of toys), a role is also played by the colour of fire. The colour red, as it turns out, plays a large role in the *Vita sexualis* of man. (One could suggest to Bloch a reference to the red light). And Bloch suggests (how persuasively is still a question!)

that there may be an associative and synaesthetic connection here.

Another researcher, Näcke,[29] sees other interpretations for pyromania. He believes that what underlies it is first and foremost phototropism, characteristic of all living matter—that is, the attracting power of bright light, the sun or fire. To this he also attributes, to a certain extent, thermotropism—that is, the magnetic power of warmth on the cells of an organism.[30]

Finally, Näcke points out also the magnetic power of the *movement* of fire:

These movements of fire are monotonous, almost rhythmic and through them, it would appear, from continual staring at fire, there gradually are formed slight circulatory disturbances in the brain which produce the same pleasant and semi-intoxicating effect as the influence of alcohol, dancing, swinging, etc. This is further assisted by the brightness, colour and outbursts of the flame . . .'

Wulffen, not entirely convincingly, wants to embrace all this under this thesis. More successful is his somewhat surprising reference to . . . Wagner: 'Richard Wagner, one of the greatest psychologists, in the monotoned, rhythmic music of *Feuerzauber* [the magic of fire] in *Die Walküre*[31] conveyed exceptionally well this stimulating and pleasant semi-intoxication which the movement of fire produces in one who watches it, the inclusion in this tonality of the theme of love between Brünnhilde and Siegfried, in combination with the image of fire and the splendid results attained by this, Wulffen then attempts to reduce entirely to erotic pre-conditions, calling Wagner 'the greatest musical sexologist.'

In no way disputing the magnificence achieved by Wagner, freely admitting to a vague connection between the element of fiery emotions and the element of fire, we are nonetheless surprised that Wulffen does not use an example that is much closer to him—one of Rachilde's novels (*Les Hors-Nature*),[32] where the doubly encountered fire is truly strictly conjugal. Where fire in the form of a double self-cremation is the sole means capable of resolving the love-conflict of the novel's heroes, who are unable to find any other way out of the created situation.

In leaving the accent on eroticism to the lot of Rachilde's novel, I should like in the case of Wagner to harp not so much upon the same pre-condition (entirely probable), but upon phenomenon of movement arising from it, and to see in it the basic attraction of 'Magic Fire' which I was called upon in production to run through my own fingers.

And this element of movement, no longer necessarily monotonous, unquestionably rhythmically essential to Wagner for the absolutely unique requirements of *Walküre* and *Siegfried*, but in the form of a wild dance by another of Wagner's characters—Loge, the God of Fire—returns us to our initial thesis: the attractiveness of fire first and foremost through its omnipotence in the realm of the creation of plastic shapes and forms.

It is no accident that the first revelations of later doctrines are seen by the majority of prophets and founders of religious philosophical teachings precisely in this fertile womb of fire.

The burning bush which appeared before Moses, the heavenly fire before Zoroaster and Buddha,[33] at the very origins of the systems which spread as though from a spark . . . it was in fire, precisely fire, according to the legends, that there were depicted the numerous quantity of future images and destinies of the teachings themselves.[34]

This same image flows like a sea of fire throughout the primary school diary of a young man who was fated, just as fantastically, to shred the destinies of nations and countries, as fantastic as the play of fire in the poetic imaginings of his youth, written by the future great man—the man who needed precisely fire, the fire that raged in the Russian capital of Moscow, to be a torch to light the path to the twilight of his glory.

The first thing written by Napoleon in the form of a story was [connected with fire].[35]

And it is no accident that another beast from the abyss, in the twilight of his declining strength, at the point of exhausted strength and imagination, at the stage of physical and moral impotence, at the zenith of disintegration of what could no longer be called a human spirit and human nature, turns precisely to fire, the fire that spreads from end to end across the eternal city—across Rome, burned to the ground with such satiety by Nero. Nero who, perhaps as a last effort, still tries to find in the tongues of the flames a play of images and themes for his soul and conscience which had faded in debauchery, waned in crime and died.

Nero sings a hymn to fire.

For a brief moment, the element of fire, through its play of images and dance of visions, is able to kindle the walking corpse of the Emperor.

But, of course, the most brilliant, the most unexpectedly rich, diverse and, at the same time, the most objectively concrete images must appear in flames not to abstract thinkers creating abstract religious systems, but above all, to artists creating real, concrete works of art.

One of them, one of the greatest artists in general, is especially deeply connected with fire. The fieriness in his struggle for the great cause of the working class, his ardour in everything concerning it, seems embodied also in his attraction to the element of fire, about which many of us heard testimony in his own words during his lifetime. One already senses that we are talking about Gorky. And it is enough to take but one of his sketches, 'Fires'[36] (or 'Fire', as it is called in another collection), in order to encounter the most colourful examples illustrating our thought:

> Great is the attraction of the magic power of fire! I have often noticed that the most self-denying people yield to the beauty of the evil play of this power, and I am not free from its influence myself. It is always a delight to me to set fire to a wood-pile, and I am just as ready to sit for days insatiably watching the flames as I am to sit and listen to music.

> The joining of fire and music here is no accident.

And, of course, herein lies one of the secrets of the attractiveness of fire for the artist. For music too is remarkable in that the images created by it flow continuously, like flame itself, eternally changeable, like the play of its tongues, mobile and endlessly diverse.

Let the libretto suggest to you that this is an ocean surf, and that—the sounds of a forest; this is a storm, and that—the play of sunlight in branches. How many varied storms and forests, suns in branches and surfs appear here to each individual imagination, how many different ones— to the same person on different days, at different hours, at different moments of his own emotional life. Music has preserved this emotional plurality of meaning in its speech, the plurality of meaning which has been displaced from language that seeks precision, distinctness, and logical exhaustion.

But it too was once like that. It did not seek precision of expression, but attempted by means of a sound-image of a word to stir the widest possible layer of emotions and associations, harmonious to this word: to convey not a precise conception, but a complex of feelings accompanying it.

This trait has been preserved in poetry. To a certain extent. To a small degree verses are dry. To a large degree they are abstract (Mallarmé).[37] But even now in the Far East, when encountering the Chinese language, the European logician, the pedant of responsible precision of language, is made indignant by this musical similarity of polysemantically flowing meaning in the elusive definition of words.

The centuries of work on language in our countries have forced this attribute out from the realm of words, but music is full of this mysterious life of not fully perceptible precise outlines of an object and image, which are just as visually captivating in the play of clouds or fire.[38]

But let us return to Gorky, to fire, and to his story, *Fires*.

It is interesting that just as headlong, at any hour of the day or night, another writer of the Russian land rushed to watch fires, a man who apparently could not be budged from his sofa by anything other than this spectacle. Could it have been in fire that he too found the outlines of the innumerable lively figures which run throughout his fables? Throughout the fables of Krylov?[39]

But let us take a look with Gorky at the swarm of fairy-tale figures which the outline of the raging and spreading flame depicts to his own creative imagination. It is curious—they almost all are in the guise of beasts. Precisely fiery tables!

He begins the sketch with an image, classical in its purity and impressiveness:

Coming, one dark February night, to the Osharsk square, I saw a frisky fox-tail of fire peep out of a garret window and shake itself in the air, speckled with large fluttering snowflakes that fell to earth slowly and unwillingly. The beauty of the fire excited me. It was as though some red beast had sprung suddenly out of the moist, tepid darkness into the window under the roof, had arched its back and was gnawing furiously at something; one could hear a dry crackling—as a bird's bones crack between one's teeth.

As I stood watching the sly artfulness of the fire I thought: Someone ought to go and knock at the windows, wake people up, and cry: 'Fire!' But I felt incapable of moving or shouting: I just stood, captivated, watching the quick growth of the flame: the hue of cock's feathers had begun to flash on the edge of the roof, the top branches of the trees in the garden became pink and golden, and the square began to light up.

The 'red rooster' of folk-sayings comes into its own. And later on, Gorky piles up page after page of ever newer and newer images which the outburst of flame blows his way.

It is curious—later on, too, almost all of them are in the guise of animals, these fiery fables. This fiery tale about the burning forests by the Volga. These images and shapes cannot be made up. They have to be seen. Read by the keen eye of the artist in the play of the element of fire.

At night, I lay on the dry, hot ground and watched the purple flames swell and balance in the sky over the forest as though bringing a sacrifice to propitiate the Wood-Goblin, incensed with thick smoke. Small, red animals jumped and crawled on the tops of the trees; bright, broad-winged birds whirled up into the smoky sky; and everywhere the fire played, full of magic and caprice. At night the forest acquired an indescribably weird, fairy-like aspect: its blue wall seemed to grow higher, and inside it, among the black trunks, the red hairy little beasts scampered wildly. They ran to the roots, and, clasping the trunks, crawled up like dexterous monkeys, struggled with one another, breaking the branches; hissed and roared and snarled; and the forest cracked as though a thousand dogs were gnawing bones.

The silhouette of the fire among the black trees changed like a kaleidoscope, and the dance of the flames was untiring and relentless. Here a large red bear of fire rolls out on the meadow, jumping clumsily and turning somersaults; losing tufts of his flaming hair, he crawls along the trunk as though to gather honey, and, reaching the top of the tree, hugs its branches in the hairy embrace of his crimson paws, balances on them, strewing pink needles in a rain of golden sparks. Now he heaves himself lightly across to the next tree, while on the one which he has left numerous blue candles light up on the bare, black branches; purple mice rush up and down the boughs, and by their rapid movements, one can see how capriciously the blue ringlets of smoke dance; hundreds of fiery ants climb up and down the bark of the trunk.

At times, the fire crept slowly out of the forest, like a cat on the lookout for a bird, and then, suddenly lifting its pointed muzzle into the air, watched as though choosing its prey. Or else another bear, a sparkling, fiery beast, would appear from the thicket and crawl on its stomach, throwing out huge paws and raking together the grass into its huge red mouth. Or else, a crowd of little dwarfs in yellow caps would come running out of the wood, followed from afar in the smoke by a dark being, tall as a mast, who marched brandishing a red banner and whistling. In light hops, like a hare, a red clod hurries away from the forest, all covered with fiery needles like a hedge-hog, flourishing a red tail of smoke behind it. And fiery worms and golden ants crawl about the trunks; red beetles wheel with dazzling wings.

The air grows more and more stifling and acrid, the smoke thick and hot; the earth smoulders, one's eyes seemed scorched, eyelashes burnt, and one can feel the hairs of one's eyebrows move with the hot blast. It is impossible to stand any longer the smoky air which tears one's lungs, yet one feels strangely unwilling to go: when shall we have the chance again to watch such a magnificent feast for fire?[40]

[The next example is from *La Débâcle* by Emile Zola.

Here we have before us the moment of culmination in the struggle of the aroused people against their enslavers.

Before us is an inverted canvas of the Apocalypse, of the downfall of the Second Empire, like Sodom and Gomorrah, symbolically perishing in the tongues of flame devouring the Tuileries Palace.

And it contains a dance of the tongues of flame which spreads into a metaphor of a fiery ball:

On the left the Tuileries was burning. By nightfall the Communards had set fire to both ends of the palace, the Pavillon de Flore and the Pavillon de Marsan, and the fire was rapidly moving towards the Pavillon de l'Horloge in the middle, where a big explosive charge had been set—barrels of powder piled up in the Salle des Maréchaux. At that moment, there were issuing from the broken windows of the connecting blocks whirling clouds of reddish smoke pierced by long blue tongues of fire. The roofs were catching, splitting open into

Grandville, 'A Female Greyhound Who Got Lost and Was Impounded'.
From *Scènes de la Vie Privée et Publique des Animaux* (1842).

Grandville, 'The Elegantly Narrow-waisted Wasps One Meets in Society'.
From *Scènes de la Vie Privée et Publique des Animaux* (1842).

blazing cracks, like volcanic earth from the pressure of the fire within.

. . . Maurice, now in the delirium of fever, gave vent to the cackle of a madman.

'Lovely party going on at the Conseil d'Etat and the Tuileries   the outside all illuminated, lustres all glittering, women dancing . . . Go on, dance in your smoking petticoats and flaming hair!'

With his good arm he sketched visions of the galas in Sodom and Gomorrah, with music, flowers and unnatural orgies, palaces bursting with such debaucheries, the disgusting nudities illuminated with such a riot of candles that they themselves were set on fire.[41]]

But whom, especially, ought flame to attract?

He, of course, who more than anyone else, lacks its fascinating traits: and foremost—freedom of transformation, freedom of the elements.

The slave of nature—primitive man, who saw in it not only the source of life's blessings, but also a symbol of easy control over all nature, where almost nothing is capable of resisting the power of fire. Is it not from here that fire worship comes?

But then also the prisoner, shackled by the weight of cruel confinement, must sense fire especially strongly as a symbol of freedom, life and power. Precisely such is the fate of yet another character from Gorky's *Fires*—the priest, Zolotnitsky.

He is imprisoned for thirty years for some sort of heretical ideas to solitary confinement in a stone cell of a monastery prison.

I myself had an occasion to see these crypt-like cells in the Prilutsk Monastery near Vologda: to survive even one night in them would already seem a feat . . . Zolotnitsky was allowed one comfort:

> During the languid course of eleven thousand days and nights, the only consolation of this captive of a Christ-loving Church, as well as his sole companion, was fire: the heretic was granted permission to light the stove of his cell unaided by others . . .

Zolotnitsky does not hold up. His reasoning becomes clouded.

He left prison a fire-worshipper, and grew animated only when he was allowed to light a wood-pile in the stove and sit in front of it, watching it. Seating himself on a low little stool, he lit the logs lovingly, making the sign of the cross over them, and murmured, shaking his head, all the words that still lived in his memory:

'Thou, who art . . . Eternal fire . . . Omnipresent . . . Omnipotent . . . Unlike anyone . . . Thy face shines throughout the ages . . . Praise and glory to Thee, Oh Burning Buohl . . .'

Not light, but precisely flame. The variability of its living forms. The diversity of flowing images read in it— that is what bewitches, attracts, fascinates.

And to encounter enslaved light, many times brighter than the fire from his stove, but shackled and deprived of movement, Zolotnitsky had to be horrified.

Zolotnitsky's horror was great when he first saw an electric lamp, when the white, bloodless light, imprisoned in the glass, flared up before him mysteriously. Having stared at it for some moments intently, the old man waved his hands in despair and began muttering plaintively: 'What! The fire imprisoned too! . . . oh—oh! . . . What for? The devil's not in it, is he? Oh—oh! Why have they done it?'

Tears streamed from his dull, colourless eyes.

He sobbed, lightly touching the shoulders of those who stood close to him with his small, dry, trembling hand: 'Oh—let it go—set it free!'

A passion for fire and its appearance is characteristic for regressive conditions and is so well-known in psychiatry, that there even exists a special euphonious term for it—'pyromania'.

I am purposely quoting from such an unspecialized work as the basic textbook, *Legal Psychiatry*:

> Pyromania is most often observed in immature, psychologically and physically underdeveloped subjects. In simple cases, the desire to commit arson can arise from a love for the spectacle of fire, not infrequently characteristic of normal people, especially children and adolescents. In pathological (sick) cases, this attraction acquires the character of an uncontrollable urge. In immature, mentally defective persons with poorly developed self-restraints, this urge can turn into action, that is, into arson . . .[42]

For a normal person, as we see, it is characteristic of the period when sensuous thought predominates—that is, in childhood. This is especially intense in pathological cases, which are characterized by higher layers of consciousness being weakened and inactive, and sensuously spontaneous reactions and urges emerging in the foreground.

All this is further characterized by the case of the fourteen-year-old girl, Sh., who was accused of setting fire to seven occupied houses—a case illustrating pyromania in the book.

From the materials of the investigation, it is clear 'that the arsons committed by her were done so without any ulterior motive.' (that is, a purely sensuous urge).

Her desire to commit arson arose in periods of a sort of unaccountable melancholy and inner unrest, during which she became irritable. It was then that the desire to see fire would arise... After having committed the arson, at the sight of fire ... she would always become calm...

The defendant comes from a hereditarily troubled family. From early childhood she was uncommunicative, whining, suffered head pains. At the age of eight, she first noticed her love for fire. She would often go into the woods to look at campfires, and when she herself built a fire, she would become happy. Later, she became irritable, fits of depression would come over her and uncontrollable, often wild urges which she 'could not suppress within [herself]. Then 'whatever comes into [her] mind, [she does], no longer able to control [herself]'. In such a condition, the defendant . . . would commit the arson.

The sight of fire evokes pleasure at the level of sensuous thought. On the other hand, the appearance of fire immerses one in sensuous thought. The urge (melancholy, etc.) is satisfied whenever a fire is lit (later—arson is committed), she becomes happy, calms down: the immersion in sensuous thought is achieved.

The defendant possesses all the corresponding prerequisites:

Together with physical underdevelopment, there was confirmed an organic affection of the central nervous system, accompanied by a slight reduction of the mental faculties. However, she is sufficiently well orientated towards everyday reality and responds critically to her situation. Her committing of arsons is explained by an uncontrollable urge to see fire, the bustle and excitement of people running towards a fire. At the sight of a blazing fire, her heart 'tickles with joy'. After the fulfilment of the urge (arson), she experiences satisfaction, accompanied by a feeling of relief and serenity.

The conclusion states:

In the cited case, there is sufficient evidence to warrant the actions of Sh. (arsons) to be regarded as actions which are unconscious, impulsive, resulting from an organic affection of the central nervous system.

Thus, we see that for an unconscious, impulsive condition, in the presence of suppressed higher nervous activity (consciousness), such a phenomenon as pyromania is characteristic and typical (in certain cases).

Consequently, persistent suggestion through fire, the appearance of fire, the play of fire, images of fire, is capable in certain cases of provoking unconscious and impulsive conditions—that is, of bringing sensuous thought' to the foreground, and forcing consciousness into the background.

Visions in fire seem to be a cradle of metonymies: in contiguity with the Tuileries Palace, they flare up into a fiery ball; in contiguity with a forest—into a swarm of animals, insects and birds.

But, irrespective of this, let us permit this swarm of animals to return us to Disney—to his central characters— to his little animals, to these great-great-grandchildren of the animal epos.

The animals in *Merbabies* substitute for other animals: fish—for mammals.

In Disney's works on the whole, animals substitute for people.

The tendency is the same: a displacement, an upheaval, a unique protest against the metaphysical immobility of the once-and-forever given.

It is interesting that the same kind of flight into an animal skin and the humanization of animals is apparently characteristic for many ages, and is especially sharply expressed as a lack of humaneness in systems of social government or philosophy, whether it is the age of American mechanization in the realm of life, welfare and morals, or the age of mathematical abstraction and metaphysics in philosophy.

It is interesting that one of the most outstanding examples of such a rebirth of the animal epos is provided precisely by the century that saw the birth of systematized metaphysics—the seventeenth century. Or more precisely, the eighteenth century, which sought to overcome it.

The French Enlightenment of the eighteenth century, in particular *French materialism*, was not only a struggle against the existing political institutions and the existing religion and theology; it was just as much an *open* struggle against *metaphysics* of the *seventeenth century*, and against all metaphysics, in particular that of *Descartes, Malebranche, Spinoza and Leibnitz.*[43]

Thus write the classics of Marxism. And I think that this is not contradicted in the present case by Hippolyte Taine, who sees in the flourishing images of the animal epos in the fables of La Fontaine,[44] a share of participation by the poet in this general protest of the eighteenth century against the seventeenth.

He writes about this in *La Fontaine et ses fables*:

What is a dog, an ant, a tree? The philosophers answered that they are machines, something like clock mechanisms which move and make noise: 'The many wheels within them take the place of man's soul; the first one moves the second, a third one follows, and finally sound is heard.' Malebranche, so tender and affectionate, beat his dog mercilessly, maintaining that it felt nothing, and that its cries were no more than wind passing through a vibrating pipe. And this was by no means a simple paradox lost in a single mind of a metaphysician. This was a general current. From a love for reasoning and discipline, the whole of man was confined to his soul, and the whole soul was allotted to reason. This reason was made an independent being, existing unto itself, separated from matter, lodged by some miracle in a body, possessing no power whatsoever over this body, supplying it with no impulses and receiving impressions from it only through the intermediary of a God called from above for the express purpose of enabling them to act upon each other. Then all beauty, all life, all nobility were given back to the human soul; empty and lowly nature was now merely a mass of pulleys and springs, as vulgar as a manufactory, unworthy of interest except for their useful products and curious at most for the moralist, who could pull from them speeches, edifying and praising their constructor. There was nothing there for a poet, he should leave animals alone and no more concern himself with carps or cows than with a wheelbarrow or mill.

His habits cut him off from them no less than his theories. For aristocrats or salon people, a weasel or a rat were no more than common and dirty creatures. A hen was a reservoir of eggs, a cow—a container of milk, a donkey was good only for carting vegetables to the market. Such creatures are not to be looked at, they are to be turned away from when they pass by; at best, they are to be laughed at and lived off as their comrades in yoke—the peasants; but they are to be walked past quickly; it would be a degradation of thought to linger on such things. These trimmed lords and ladies who spend their lives pretending, feel at ease only between sculptured panelling and before glittering mirrors; if they set foot upon the ground, then it must be a well-swept lane; if they tolerate the woods and waters, then they are the waters spouting from the mouths of bronze monsters; they are woods lined with hornbeams. They care for nature only when transformed into a garden.

As the eighteenth century advanced, rules became more strict, language was refined, pretty replaced beautiful; etiquette defined more precisely the slightest movement and conversation; a code was established which instructed the proper way to sit and to dress, to make a tragedy and a speech, to fight and to love, to die and to live: so well that literature became a machine of phrases, and man—a doll for curtseys. Rousseau, who first protested and declaimed against this restrictive and artificial life, appeared to have discovered nature—La Fontaine, without protesting or declaiming, discovered it before him.[45]

That which Rousseau denounced through overt polemics and slogans, the works of La Fontaine had already said through artistic image and form:

'He defended his animals from Descartes, who made machines of them. He does not dare to philosophize like the doctors, he asks permission; he hazards his idea as a timid supposition, he attempts to invent a soul for the use of rats and rabbits.' Moreover: '... Like Virgil, he too felt sorry for trees; he did not exclude them from life. "Plants breathe," he said. At the same time that an artificial civilization was clipping the yews and hornbeams of Versailles into cones and geometrical figures, he wanted to preserve the freedom of their branches and their foliage.'[46]

The heartless geometrizing and metaphysics here give rise to a kind of antithesis, an unexpected rebirth of universal animism.

Animism, in which there wander vague ideas and sensations of the interconnection of all elements and kingdoms of nature, long before science guessed the configuration of this connection in sequence and stages. Hand in hand with it went also an objective understanding of surrounding nature.

Before this, man had known no other way than the supplying of the environment with its own soul and judgement by analogy with himself.

Even the ancient Chinese held forth on this:

The Happiness of Fish

'Chuang Tzu and Hui Tzu were strolling along the dam of the Hao River when Chuang Tzu said, "See how the minnows come out and dart around where they please! That's what fish really enjoy!"

'Hui Tzu said, "You're not a fish—how do you know what fish enjoy?"

'Chuang Tzu said, "You're not I, so how do you know I don't know what fish enjoy?"

'Hui Tzu said, "I'm not you, so I certainly don't know what you know. On the other hand, you're certainly not a fish—so that still proves you don't know what fish enjoy!"

'Chuang Tzu said, "Lets go back to your original question, please. You asked me how I know what fish enjoy—so you already knew I knew it when you asked the question. I know it from my own happiness in standing here beside the Hao."'[47]

None of this, however, prevents La Fontaine from observing in the keenest way his characters in real life. Their humanization in no way hinders this. Perhaps even the opposite. Let us recall Grandville,[48] for example, where human nature is absolutely indissolubly interwoven with an image of animals:

Once when he (La Fontaine) was to dine at the house of Mme Harvey, he got held up and only arrived close to midnight. He had been enjoying himself following an ant funeral all the way to the burial grounds, then he had accompanied the cortège back to theirhole...[49]

This accounts for such a knowledge of the life, habits and behaviour of animals, which involuntarily form an image and personality resembling man. This accounts for such a skilful assignment of roles: the Ant (in French the word is feminine), even in its appearance—dry, lean, thin-waisted and dressed in black—bears a resemblance, of course, to a tireless housekeeper, thrifty and businesslike. Frogs are usually given stupid roles: but having gazed into their round, vacant eyes, its impossible not to agree with such a role assignment.

This knowledge of animals is often lacking in other fabulists. Florian[50] was far from always successful in casting animals for the right roles. He will either give affectionate, brotherly feelings and sensitivity to a silly and too coquettish bird, or make a rabbit a romantic dreamer, worthy of elegies. The speeches of such a rabbit not only come off as rhetoric, but are completely out of keeping with the disposition of a rabbit: quick, frivolous, gluttonous, and a very poor father.

Such misses are not to be found in either La Fontaine or Disney. It is enough to listen closely to Goofy's guttural sounds of self-satisfaction, to look closely at the gluttonous, loutish behaviour of Donald, or to admire the gliding gait of a Swedish skater in the movements of Wilbur the grasshopper along the surface of water—not to mention the carefree gaiety of *The Three Little Pigs*—in order to be convinced how much to the point, appropriate and in character they are all selected.

But that is not all. A certain foreign critic correctly noticed yet another trait: Mickey, not only in his personality, but even anatomically, is consistent—on his paws, as is the case with mice, there are not five human fingers, but four, wearing white gloves.

It is interesting the degree to which this does not hinder the rich fantasy of transformations, which the author of Mickey possesses: how easily and gracefully these four fingers on both of Mickey's hands, playing a Hawaiian guitar, suddenly dissolve into two pairs of extremities. The two middle fingers become little legs, the two outer fingers —little hands. And suddenly there are no longer two hands, but two funny, little white people, elegantly dancing together along the strings of the Hawaiian guitar.[51]

And I should like to repeat about Disney, the words with which Taine concludes his comparison with Buffon[52] in favour of La Fontaine:

He achieves effects that Buffon does not . . . A mass of observations are assembled within him, imperceptible even to himself, and form a unique impression, as waters rushing from all directions flood into a reservoir, from which they leave for another voyage and along a different course. He saw the attitudes, the gaze, the fur, the dwelling, the shape of a fox or weasel, and the emotion produced by the combination of all these perceptible details engenders within him a moral character complete with all its traits and inclinations. He does not copy, he translates. He does not transcribe what he has seen, he invents based upon what he has seen. He condenses and he deduces. He transposes, and this is the most precise word; for he transports into one world what he has seen in another, into the spiritual world, what he has seen in the physical world. The zoologist and orator attempt, by means of enumeration and grouping, to give us an ultimate sensation; he installs himself from the very first in this sensation in order to develop further ones within us. They clamber step by step towards the top; he places himself naturally upon this top, and every step he takes is towards a superior domain, to which this is but the stepping stone. They learn, and he

knows; they prove, and he sees. This is how a fabulist can be at the same time and in the same place
both a painter of animals and a painter of men.
The mixture of human nature, far from concealing
animal nature, gives it relief; it is in the transformation of beings that poetry gives the most
precise idea of them; it is through altering them,
that poetry expresses them; it is because poetry
is the freest inventor, that it is the most faithful
imitator.[53]

The principle of poetry is to transform, to convert.

In comedy, this 'principle' becomes action.

In Shakespeare's tragedies, people change. In his comedies, the characters are transformed constantly . . . by
disguising themselves, or undergoing physical transformation through magical means.

In Disney—they turn into each other. One of the
devices of comedy is the literalization of a metaphor.

Thus, a master's 'eyes and ears'—a traditional
metaphor for a detective and spy, whether in Greek theatre
or in scandalous literature of the eighteenth century—
appear in comic form in one case as . . . the last names of
their authors, and in another—in Aristophanes—as funny
masks, representing a single gigantic eye, and a single
gigantic ear.

That is why poetry's principle of transformation works comically in Disney, given as a literal metamorphosis . . .

Metamorphosis is not a slip of the tongue, for in leafing through Ovid, several of his pages seem to be copied from Disney's cartoons.[54]

[*10 January 1942*]

We are consciously limiting ourselves to three complete 'analogies' in theme and form to Disney: Lewis Carroll's *Alice*, Andersen's *Tales*, La Fontaine's *Fables*. An analogy of the 'resurrection' of the natural, the animal (not in the sense of 'beast', but in the sense of '*das Animalische*' [the animal]) as antitheses: La Fontaine to the seventeenth century (H. Taine), Andersen to the eighteenth (Brandes), *Alice* to the nineteenth, Disney to the twentieth.

N.B. Rousseau—*Paul et Virginie*[55]—Andersen. Andersen complete in pure form the line of this tendency from the end of the eighteenth century. La Fontaine pioneers for the seventeenth century. Lewis Carroll is an antithesis to industrialized, positivistic England (Dickens as well).

They are also interesting as interstages. The a-moralism of Carroll (pure fantasy). The semi-moralism of Andersen (not always pure fantasy). The moralism of La Fontaine (rational fantasy). That is, the percentage of the conscious and tendentiously directed element in each is different. It is quite interesting that Disney is still further form consciousness than perhaps even Carroll. That is, the tendency of the prevailing of pre-logic (its deepening and expansion) precisely echoes the growth of the opposite wing: Descartes—Voltaire—industrial England (Kant)—industrial America. This crescendo of the rational is echoed by a 'degradation' into the pre-logical: La Fontaine—Andersen —Carroll—Disney. A reverse crescendo of purity of pre-logical method runs towards the very most primal.]

III

Alma-Ata, 4 November 1941

A new setting dictates a new modus in which to work: there is no material to quote from on hand. The modus is prompted by *Ivan the Terrible*. There, it is done this way–episode follows episode, and all the *Beleg-Material* [supporting material] of ideas is *als Anhang* [like an appendix]. Perhaps there is an outlet and salvation in this: in Moscow, I was drowning in citations. Perhaps this new approach will help to focus correctly the essence of the ideas, and it will be possible to embellish in an appendix. It is funny—I am writing in the same small handwriting that I used during the Civil War! The identicalness of setting engenders, etc? Put more simply—no paper.

Walt Disney's work is the most omni-appealing I have ever met.

It is justifiable to suppose that this work has most or all the traits of pre-logical attractiveness.

Let us consider the traits characteristic of his work and decipher them.

First, let us enumerate the traits found in Disney's pictures:

They are animated drawings.

Stroke drawings.

Humanized animals.

Further animated[56] (with humanlike souls).

Absolutely synaesthetic (audio-visually).

Metamorphic, and again in two (both) senses—both as subject and as form:

Things like *Merbabies* (octopuses playing elephants, the striped goldfish—a tiger).

The primal plasmatic origin, i.e. the use of polyformic capabilities of an object: fire, assuming all possible guises.

Does not the attractiveness of fire lie in this, and one of the mysteries of fire-worship?

This is substantiated in Gorky (*Fires*), where fire takes the form of beasts.

Also in relation to form as such: from this comes the writhing that is typical of Disney—a plasmaticness of contour.

Disney and *Alice*—necks, sizes, etc.

Not just the animal world, but also the plant world.

••

A deciphering of all these individual traits.

••

About the animal epos. Totemism. About 'reverting into a beast' as the idea of strength through the *pars pro toto* of wearing horns (ancient weapons); this is on an ironic plane (i.e. reversed 180 degrees) in 'horn-wearers' [cuckolds]— as the 'wearers' of impotence! (N.B. Here belong bestial *Schimpfwörter* [terms of abuse]—obviously as a twist on the earlier, magical extolment of a quality through appellations: *Coeur de Lion*, etc.).

In terms of their material, Disney's pictures are pure ecstasy—all the traits of ecstasy (the immersion of self in nature and animals)

Their comicality lies in the fact that the process of ecstasy is represented as an object: literalized, formalized.

That is, Disney is an example (within the general formula of the comical) of a case of *formal ecstasy*. (Producing an effect of the same degree of intensity as ecstasy!).

America and the *formal logic of standardization* had to give birth to Disney as a natural reaction to the pre-logical.

In the history of literature and art, this is not the first time, similar traits of past ages gave birth to quite similar phenomena.

Such was the case with La Fontaine as a protest against the logic of Cartesian philosophy.

This was brilliantly demonstrated by H. Taine (*La Fontaine et ses fables*).

Something less splendid also appears in the period of scholasticism, when an outlet from the pincers of the logic of ideas also proceeds along some similar 'bestial' paths.

••

The *Batrachomyomachia*.[57]

••

Kinderspiele [children's toys] as beasts—this is a station on the way—a phylogenetic repetition.

Metamorphoses is a direct protest against the standardly immutable.

••

The *stroke drawing*, as a line, with only one contour, is the very earliest of drawing—cave drawings.

In my opinion, this is not yet a consciously creative act, but the simple automatism of outlining a contour. It is a roving eye, from which movement the hand has not yet been separated (into an independent movement).

This is preceded by the stage when simply the whole man encircles an object, making a drawing with himself (there is an element of this in the Acropolis).

The silhouette drawing has its own attractiveness, evidently on the basis of this (cf. Japanese silhouettes as such in the book of silhouettes).[58]

Mobility of contour is still a certain link with the past in the sense that then, drawing was fundamentally (and almost exclusively) running, a movement which was as if only accidentally erased.

It is especially notable that Norwegian cave drawings are approximately the *natural size* of deer and other models (i.e. even in scale, an untouched, direct impression.

See the data on this in the corresponding volume of *Propyläen-Kunstgeschichte*.)[59]

The animated drawing is the most direct manifestation of animism. That which is known to be lifeless, a graphic drawing, is animated.

Drawing as such—outside an object of representation—is brought to life.

But furthermore and inseparably, the subject—the object of representation is also animated. Ordinary lifeless objects, plants, beasts—all are animated and humanized.

There occurs the process of the mythological personification of phenomena of nature (a forest as a wood-goblin, a house as a house-spirit) in the image and likeness of man.

From an unexpected shock, a man bumps into a chair in the dark —you regress to the stage of sensuous thought. You curse the chair as thought it were a living being.

Here, seeing a chair as a living being, or a dog as a human, you fly headlong into emotions of a psychical change—a shock, into the blissful state of the sensuous stage.

The audio-visual synaesthetics are obvious and speak for themselves.[60]

The very idea, if you will, of the animated cartoon is like a direct embodiment of the method of animism. Whether a momentary supplying of an inanimate object with life and a soul, which we also preserve when we bump into a chair and curse it as though it were a living being, or whether a long-term supplying with life, with which primitive man endows inanimate nature.

And thus, what Disney does is connected with one of the deepest-set traits of man's early psyche.[61]

In his article 'Typical Development of Religious-Mythological Creativity', Evgeni Kagarov cites curious data on the external appearance of the soul in folk beliefs:

Among the most common conceptions of the external appearance and form of the soul are the following:

Breath, smoke, steam, wind, fog, clouds.

Animals, especially birds and insects; among reptiles—snakes. Recently the Russian scholar, V. P. Klinger, in his work, *Animals in Ancient and Contemporary Superstition* (Kiev, 1911), outlined beautifully the role of the concept of the animal-soul in folk belief, ritual and, to some extent, poetry at various times and among different peoples. Separating animals by class and searching for motives in their respective comparisons with the human soul, the researcher arrives at the conclusion that the linking conceptions here were:

Wind, as one of the most frequent images of the soul (birds, winged insects, fleet-footed animals such as deer and horses).

Earth, as the dwelling-place of the dead (reptiles, rodents, ants).

Night, as the time when the dead walk the earth (nocturnal beasts: the wolf, the lion) and, finally,

Fire, as the other equally widespread image of the soul (the rooster and the chicken).[62]

N.B. Birds—'sky words'.[63] The initial metonymy at the basis is quite obvious.

Fire-beast (in superstition): Tylor, cf. *Primitive Culture*:

In various forms and under several names, the Fire-god is known. Nowhere does he carry his personality more distinctly than under his Sanskrit name of Agni, a word which keeps its quality, though not its divinity, in the Latin ignis. The name of Agni is the first word of the first hymn of the Rig-Veda: 'Agni I entreat, divine appointed priest of sacrifice!' The sacrifices which Agni receives go to the gods, he is the mouth of the gods, but he is no lowly minister, as it is said in another hymn: 'No god indeed, no mortal is beyond the might of thee, the mighty one, O Agni!'

The Carinthian peasant will add fodder to the fire to re-kindle it, and throw lard or dripping to it, that it may not burn down his house.

To the Bohemian it is not right to throw away the crumbs after a meal, for they belong to the fire.[64]

For bestial metaphors in a description of fire, cf. Gorky's *Fires*.

They are interesting in their transitivity from action (fire-devourer), to an association with plastic-form (the fox-tail of fire).

Among the descriptions of fire-worship in Asia, we can point to the story of Jonas Hanway from his *Travels* of 1740, about the 'everlasting fire at the burning wells near Baku, on the Caspian...'[65]

The attractiveness of fire lies in its infinite changeability, modulation, transitivity and the continuous coming into being of images.

Thus, fire is like an embodiment of the principle of eternal coming into being, the eternally life-producing womb and omnipotence. In this sense, it also resembles the potentiality of the primal plasma, from which everything can arise.

The very enumeration of the traits of fire, as an object of contemplation, demonstrates how close its attributes are to the principles governing the Universe—the principles of dialectics.

Fire as a spectacle, a spectacle which is not bound by the question of good or evil, a spectacle of aesthetic *an und für sich* [in and of itself] contemplation, assembled, as it were, according to a dialectical formula (just like ecstatic compositions). In Gorky's summary of the aesthetics of fire in *Fires* through individual stories, it's as if there were strewn the theses of the aesthetic system of fire.

From the precondition of a release from the problem of fire to *an und für sich* worshipper of fire (the fire-setter, free from moral restraints).

To the strict division of the element of fire from light: for example, in the story (I would say, in the 'allegory') about the old monk imprisoned in the monastery and the electric light bulb (in which the god of fire has been chained). The erotic element of fire. German sexologists, naturally, make this interpretation. The statistics on young girls in the period of *Pubertät*, especially inclined to arson—'in their blood burns the *fires* of desires'—the *ardour* of love.

I think all this is, as always, 'way stationing' on eroticism.

For eroticism is the cheapest (and the most readily available) means of attaining ecstasy. A connection is made between fire and Eros—or rather, they should be connected not directly, but through a common, general third—ecstasy as such. In both, there is the formula of *des grossen Mysteriums der Entstehung* [the great mystery of genesis]. Notwithstanding the complete absence of any casual connection between them or any kind of genetic connection, etc. It's simply that both, like so much else, *zielt in denselben Kern* [aim towards the same core], and it appears that they have a direct connection.

Freud makes the same mistake when he interprets dreams as a sign of sexual dissatisfaction—and hence, supposedly . . .

Ecstasy is a sensing and experiencing of the primal omnipotence —the element of coming into being—the 'plasmaticness' of existence, from which everything can arise.

And it is beyond any image, without an image, beyond tangibility, much like a pure sensation.

In order to capture this sensation, man searches for an image with traits capable of resembling this state and sensation. This image will then be linked to an idea, a verbal sensation, a communication, a story about this state.

Thus, there will phenomena with polyformic capabilities: the ever changing (1) appearance of fire (the poet Gorky after the prophet Moses!), (2) plasmatic, inconstant form, (3) water (water becoming a boxing glove), (4) clouds (all four concepts are in Disney), (5) music: but fire for Gorky is music!

In many respects, herein also lies the secret of the fascination of music, for its image too is not stable.

The arising images are different for everyone (depending on the base community), different for the same listener in different moods, and the sensation of multi-diversity is one of its fascinations.

But they are equated, music and fire, by the fire-worshipper Gorky:

Great is the attraction of the magic power of fire! I have often noticed that the most self-denying[66] people yield to the beauty of the evil play[67] of this power, and I am not free from its influence myself. It is always a delight to me to set fire to a wood-pile, and I am just as ready to sit for days insatiably watching the flames as I am to sit and listen to music.[68]

27 December 1941

It is interesting that what primitive man has in superstition (Agni), the poet (Gorky) has in images.

In the philosopher, it turns out to be an emblem expressing the very same sensation, the same thought, but through a philosophical generalization.

Three philosophers agree on this: Heraclitus, Hegel (who speaks of Heraclitus) and Lenin, who excerpts the following passage in *The Conspectus of Hegel's 'Lectures on the History of Philosophy'* (cf. *Philosophical Notebooks*).[69]

In regard to the fact that Heraclitus considered fire as a process, Hegel says: 'Fire is physical time, it is absolute unrest.'

But what is time?

Heraclitus said: 'die Zeit ist das erste körperliche Wesen' (time is the first corporeal essence).

Lenin considers the expression, 'corporeal'—'unfortunate', but he says, time is 'the first sensuous essence.'

Hegel says of time: 'Time is pure Coming into Being, as perceived.'

Hegel must be studied.

Heraclitus must be studied.

Anyhow:

... fire is a process ...

... fire is physical time ...

... time is the first sensuous essence ...

... time is pure coming into being ...

There we are:

Fire is an image of coming into being, revealed in a process.

'Absolute unrest' is obviously a designation for the womb of the birth of 'all-(omni-)possible phenomena and forms'.

Ergo, there is nothing on earth as attractive as this.

Engels par excellence; he sees each phenomenon in the dynamics of the process of coming into being—both the system of philosophy, and landscape.[70] Sensing the unity of the whole system of the world just as keenly as a poet, the correspondence or the difference of its diversity. Hence, the amazing ability to equate movements of this basis.

A tremor of contour is a tremor of the author, like the tremor of the visible in a pure aspect.

Later, a derivative.

The rhythm of your experience is the basis of the rhythm of your construction.

(My *On the Structure of Things*).[71]

These stretching necks, etc. Disney again, directly and spontaneously.

But still another trait—the plasmaticness of form, as such.

The next stage in metaphor is metaphor in form and objects.

Here, there is not longer a projection of self onto an object or from an object on to self, but a transference from object to object.

But the process occurs not in comparisons and parallelism, as Veselovsky[72] writes, but again according to the laws of sensuous thought: by the identicalness of the emotional (affective) perception from both these and others.

Thus, 'a deer is corn' arises on the basis of the fact that both nourish (Lévy-Bruhl).[73] As such, they can be derived from movement. In such cases, an identicalness of the motor outline of the visual perception of form (or of the movements of different objects) evokes an identical perception of movement, and by the principle of *pars pro toto*, an equal sign is placed between the entire phenomena to which they belong.

But the most interesting thing, of course, is the apparent reversion to the primal state on the very highest levels.

Over time, a dynamic picture may become complex, and whole systems of thought may, in a sufficiently comprehensive and full consciousness (i.e. equally logical and pre-logically figurative), result in striking comparisons on the basis of the dynamic picture.

Such synthetic consciousnesses were the classics of Marxism, which commanded a living synthesis of both sources of thought in dialectics.

THE ANIMAL EPOS[74]
[*Alma-Ata, November 1941*]

Man in an image—in the form of an animal.

The most literal expression of any poeticization, of any form: the difference of levels between form and content.

The form of an animal is evolutionarily a step backwards in relation to its content, to man.

In psychology, 'don't arouse the beast in me'—i.e. the early complex—this always takes place.

Here, it is brought to the surface and to the touch!

Compare Totemism and Darwinism—descent from animals.

Totemism [passes through three stages]

The first stage:

The unity of man and animal (the evolutionary stage). 'Factual' metempsychosis and the belief in the migration of souls.[75]

The second stage:

The unity of man and animal in totemistic belief.

The third stage:

The comparison of man with animal—the metaphoric series.

Cf. Below: Veselovsky (p. 193)—examples from Homer.

In this sense, Disney is on the Homeric stage: his beasts are metaphoric to people, i.e. reversed to the comparison of man with animal. They are plastic metaphors in essence.

The gamecock is a plastic metaphor of an aggressive, cocky fighter. Taken in reverse and literally.

The point here, of course, is still more profound:

We compare a fighter to a cock, for boxing, both as a sport and as a spectacle (there is no difference of principle: the viewer helps the boxers along. Note how exhausting is the spectacle of boxing—muscular exhaustion, and not

from the tension of attention), is an activity of the aggressive, cock-like level. That is, the animal-sensuous level.

This last (a duelling activity even of animals) is rooted,
of course, still deeper:

It is the concentrated, primal, physiological, biological,
magnetic and other reciprocal influence of oppositions.

The comical device of the literalization of a metaphor
rests upon the archaism of the absence of a transference
and figurative sense, that is, the pre-metaphoric (metaphor: transfer) stage. (Why the effect is comical is seen in
a separate excursus).

The second stage

'A folk tale from Annam (probably of Chinese origin): once a childless man wanted to eat a huge
eel that lived in a spot where several rivers con-
verged. A bonze appeared and asked him not to
touch the eel. Seeing that his appeals were in vain,
the bonze asked if he could have something to eat
before he left, to which the man agreed. When he
cooked the eel, there appeared in it the food he
had given the bonze. He then realized that the
bonze was none other than an apparition of the
eel itself' (Veselovsky, *Historical Poetics*, p. 533).

[In specialist literature on the subject, one of the Indian tribes of northern Brazil I soften cited as an example.

The Indians of this tribe, the Bororo, maintain, for example that although they are people, they are at the same time, a particular species of red parrot that is found widely in Brazil. They do not mean by this that they will turn into these birds after death, nor that their ancestors were once parrots. Nothing of the sort. They assert directly that they really are these very birds. This is not a question of similarity of names or ancestry, but a full simultaneous identity of both.][76]

The next level within this stage is mixed: no longer a simultaneous double existence, but (1) descent from an animal (totemic); (2) mating with animals; (3) animal wet nurses; (4) animal helpers.[77]

All four cases are in the nature of a gradual moving away from joint existence.

Finally, the 'animal helper' turns into descriptive characterizations of help—epithet, metaphor, comparison, revealing the next stage-category.

The third stage

The more ancient the epos, the less man is separated from animal, the closer he is to him, and the more abundant and splendid the comparison with beasts and animals.

I am citing an excerpt taken by Veselovsky from Homer (in reference to something else) in his work, *Psychological Parallelism and its Forms Reflected in Poetic Style* (1898):[78]

There is a scent of something archaic from the comparison of Sigurd with a deer (*Gudrun*, II, 2,5), of Helga with its dew-covered calf, antlers glistening in the sunlight, while he himself towers above all other beasts or Agamemnon with a great bull standing out from the rest of the grazing flock (*Iliad*, II, 480); the two Aiantes, standing together in battle—with a pair of bulls in a yoke (*Il.*, XIII, 703); the Trojans following their commanders—with a flock being led to trough by a ram (*Il.*, XIII, 429); Odysseus with a fat ram (*Il.*, III, 196); the Myrmidons, heading courageously for battle, recall wasps descending upon a little boy who has destroyed their nest (*Il.*, XVI, 641); the men who fall upon the body of Sarpedon (*Il.*, XVI, 641; II, 469), with flies buzzing around a milk-filled saucer; the courage instilled in Menelaus by Athene (*Il.*, XVII, 570), with the courage of a fly, constantly shooed and still descending upon a man in order to feast upon his blood; while the Trojans who flee from Achilles to Xanthus, are compared with locusts, escaping from fire into a river, or with a fish fleeing from a dolphin (*Il.*, XXI, 12, 22).

Odysseus bears malice towards the maids who pander to Penelope's suitors: such as the animosity of a dog guarding his pups (*Odyssey*, XX, 14); Menelaus guards the body of Patroclus, ready to ward off attack, as a cow will not leave its first-born calf (*Il.*, XVII,14). (N.B. Achilles?). When the Aiantes, dragging the body of Patroclus, remind the singer (*Il.*, XVII, 743) of two mules dragging a mast tree from a mountain; when Aias yields reluctantly before the onslaught of the Trojans, like a stubborn ass who has wandered into a field and will not yield to the blows that little boys shower upon him (*Il.*, XI, 558)—we shall not understand the meaning of these images if we do not remember that in Homeric poems, an ass does not appear in the typical light we are accustomed to, which we attribute, for example, to the images of a sheep and goat; whereas in the *Iliad* (IV, 433), the murmur of the Trojan army is compared with the bleating of sheep in a rich man's pen; the Trojans—with bleating goats, afraid of a lion (*Il.*, XI, 383); the joy of his comrades at the sight of Odysseus returning from Circe—with the joy of calves leaping towards their mother coming back from the field, and running around her with moos (*Od.*, X, 410).

The *Rig Veda* went even further, comparing the beauty of a song with the mooing of a dairy cow, just as in one quatrain of *Hâla* it is said that to divert one's eyes from a beautiful girl is just as difficult as it is for a feeble cow to get out of silt in which it is stuck. All this was just as natural as the images of the killing or killed animals, which the death of this or that hero suggested to Homer (*Il.*, XVII, 522; *Od.*, XX, 389; *Il.*, XVI, 407); when for example, the companions of Odysseus, captured by Scylla, are compared with fish pulled from the water and quivering on the bank (*Od.*, XII, 251).

Etc. ad infinitum.

Such is the stage where the 'animalization' (the opposite process to the 'personification' of an ape, moving forward) of man, with the effect of the reconstruction of the sensuous system of thought, occurs not through identification (cf. the second stage—Bororo), but through likening.

The sensuous effect is obtained only when there is a sensuous immersion in the likened subject.

This is critical in the substitution of man by an animal, and of an animal by man.

The unexpectedness for us of such a-poetical comparisons (a cow, a sheep, a fly) stems from the fact that here, the estimation of an animal is made in terms of its basic economic value. (A cow for nourishment, sheep for wool and so on.)

For a society with a sufficient table of ranks, such as the Greeks, this is an obvious survival (but poetry is always a step behind in the consciousness) of the stage when there was no such table of ranks—a moral, aesthetic, even class table relating to phenomena of nature. Precious and base metals are a reflection of a class-differentiating society. So are a 'beast of burden' and a 'free falcon'.

Also in terms of aesthetic appraisal:

A cow is first and foremost a wet nurse, and the aesthetic appraisal of its gracefulness (less than that of a fallow deer) does not yet figure.

The same for a sheep.

There are no ranks. Each animal is considered directly in terms of its usefulness, its necessity.

Even the fly is valued for its qualities useful for borrowing: for example, persistence from its position, and not pestiness from ours.

What is completely lacking is a moment of reverse projection of the elements of man and his traits on to animals.

We have already discussed the social theories. The moral theories also. When man's individual traits prove to be not unique and exclusive, but the leading traits for a whole species of animal: the courage of a snow leopard, the craftiness of a fox, the dirtiness of a pig (although it is in a puddle for reasons of hygiene and to get rid of possible parasites). The stubbornness of an ass, the slow-wittedness of a sheep.

This trait of reverse projection has the same pre-stage in myths of the embodiment of people in animals. Directly.

And therefore, the personification of animals in this moralizing, fabulist manner, has as a sensuously nourishing subtext its own offshoot of totemistic belief in the factual regression into an animal.

Cf. Veselovsky, *Poetics of Plots* (1897–1906): 'The transformation into beasts and plants in myths and folk tales, as the reverse process of totemistic concepts.'[79]

Through this method of the personification of an animal, Disney directly, plastically and effectively achieves the embodiment of that which exists in the Bororos' beliefs:

the Indians of the Bororo tribe believe that they are simultaneously both humans and red parrots—their totemic beast. The peacock and parrot, the wolf and horse, the night stand and dancing flame of Disney are actually simultaneously and identically both an animal (or object, or bird) and a human.

The formula of the Bororos, incomprehensible to the conscious, logical mind, but clear to sensuous thought, becomes tangible and effective in Disney's parrot, and, of course, completely immerses us in the system of sensuous thought.

Animism

I am taking the definition by Veselovsky from his article, 'Psychological Parallelism and Its Forms Reflected in Poetic Style' (N.B. I conduct a polemic on the subject of parallelism with Veselovsky elsewhere—here, I am using only the factual material of the cited illustrations and the general ideas which are indisputable):

Man assimilates images of the external world in forms of his self-consciousness; especially primitive man who has not yet developed habits of abstract, non-figurative thought, although the latter can never occur without a certain degree of figurativeness. We involuntarily transfer onto nature our experience of life, which is expressed in movement, in the manifestation of a force directed by a will; in phenomena or objects in which movement was detected, there were suspected at one time or another signs of energy, will, life. This view of the world, we call animistic.[80]

(The definition by Lévy-Bruhl—'participational,' and other definitions resulting from the idea that a non-differentiating consciousness reflects a non-differentiated social environment, I like more. Cite them.).[81]

This view of the world 'rests upon a comparison of subject and object on the basis of the category of movement'. (N.B. There is not yet a comparison. For there is not yet a differentiation of the subjective and the objective. And it's from here that the animation of nature arises: I and nature are one and the same, later on—identical, still later—alike. Before the stage of a sense of—difference, they all work towards the animation of nature, towards animism. This needs to be outlined very distinctly and sharpened in principle.)

On the basis of the category of movement, or action, as a sign of volitional, vital activity. Animals, naturally, were seen as objects; they most of all recalled man; here was the distant psychological basis of the animal apologist; but plants, too, pointed to the same resemblance. They too were born and blossomed, matured and bent against the wind. The sun also appeared to move—it rose and set, the wind chased clouds, lightning rushed along, fire enveloped, devoured branches, etc. The inorganic, immobile world was involuntarily drawn into this series. It too lived.[82]

In English, Disney's moving drawing is called an animated cartoon.

And in this name, both concepts are interwoven—both animateness (anima, soul) and mobility (animation, liveliness, mobility).

Even this condition of the indissolubleness (the unity) an animatedness and movement is already profoundly atavistic and completely in accord with the structure of primitive thought.

I myself had occasion to write about this with respect to material of Norse mythology—about this unity in connection with the divine functions, which the Nordic world attributed to the Father of the Gods—Odin-Wotan, this product of the animization of the forces of nature.

In my article, 'The Incarnation of Myth', I wrote in regard to my staging of Wagner's *Die Walküre* in the Bolshoi Theatre:[83]

Wotan was given the element of Air. But since this element can only be perceived when it is in motion, Wotan also personifies movement in general. Movement in all its variety—from the mildest breath of a breeze to the tempestuous rage of a storm.

But the consciousness that created and bore myths was not able to distinguish between direct and figurative understanding. Wotan, who personified movement in general and primarily the movement of the forces of nature, at the same time embodied the whole compass of spiritual movements: the tender emotions of those in love; the lyrical inspiration of a singer and a poet or, equally, the warlike passions of soldiers and the courageous fury of the heroes of yore.

From the very same principle comes the idea: if it moves then it is alive; i.e. moved by an innate, independent, volitional impulse

The degree to which—not in a logically conscious aspect, but in a sensuously perceiving one—we too are subject every minute to this very same phenomenon, becomes evident from our perception of the living drawings of none other than Disney.

We know that they are drawings, and not living beings.

We know that they are projections of drawings on a screen.

We know that they are miracles and tricks of technology, that such beings do not really exist.

But at the same time:

We sense them as alive.

We sense them as moving, as active.

We sense them as existing and even thinking.

And from the very same sphere of this stage of thought also comes the animization of immobile objects of nature like everyday objects and the lines of landscape.

The eye of the observer (the subject) 'runs round' the observed (the object). The very term 'runs round'—preserves within it the preceding stage when the comprehension of an object was made with the arms, and the 'running round' took place with the legs moving around the object not comprehended by the arms. Then this process was concentrated into comprehension through a glance—a glance 'running round' the object.

The difference from the preceding case consists of the fact that here the subject (eye) moves along the outlines of the object (thing), and not the object (thing) itself is moving in space.

But, as is well known, at this stage of development there is yet no differentiation between the subjective and the objective. And the movement of an eye, running along the line of a mountain's contour, is read just as easily as the running of the contour itself.

The eye glances off in the direction of a road, and this is read just as easily as the road itself moving off into the distance.

Thus, in a linguistic metaphor which also arises from this process, and exists as traces of this stage of thought in the fabric of language the process consists of the fact that in a number of cases, the action of glancing itself (which has already figuratively transferred the actions of man, the whole of man, onto itself, as a part of man) is 'animistically' ascribed to the object of observation.

I am citing a number of examples from Veselovsky, which I happen to have to hand:[84]

'Un parc immense *grimpait* la côte ...'

(Daudet, *L'Évangéliste*, ch. VI).

'*Behaglich streckte* dort das Land *sich*

In Eb'nen aus, weit, endlos weit ...

Hier *stieg es plötzlich* und *entschlossen*

Empor, stets *kühner* himmelan...'

(Lenau, *Wanderung im Gebirge*)

'*Sprang* über's ganze Haideland

Der *junge* Regenbogen...'

(Lenau, *Die Haideschenke*)

'Fernhin *schlich das hagre Gebirg*, wie ein wandelnd Gerippe,

Streckt das Dörflein *vernügt* über die Wiesen sich aus'
(Hölderlin)

'Der Himmel glänzt in reinstem Frühlingslichte,

Ihm schwillt der Hügel sehnsuchtsvoll entgegen ...'

(Möricke, *Zu viel*)

The process of formations is quite apparent.

The eye leaps, creeps over, skips. On the basis of the characteristic of this one trait of movement, its outline, rhythm, pattern—in accordance with the law of *pars pro toto*—there is reconstructed the full act of the leaping, creeping, skipping of the whole man.

Through an identification of subject and object, or rather through the indivisibleness of the two for this stage—all these movements and actions are ascribed to the landscape itself, to the hill, hamlet, mountain chain, etc.

This kind of motor metaphor (transfer is a later process, capable of being carried out, and mainly of acting, but only because of this prerequisite, earlier condition, affective identicalness, identicalness of affect) is the very earliest, most ancient type of metaphor—directly motory. (Thus the Father of the Gods, Wotan, is Movement).

It is verbal, active, a process, but not objective.

Not objectively visible, even less 'a comparison of something with something' (two objective phenomena between each other, which would already be a later stage) —but rather a motori-subjectively sensed metaphor, par excellence.

This is so true that Chamberlain (*Goethe*),[85] for example, overlooks this type of comparison. For example, he considers that for Goethe and Goethe's realistic greatness, there is a characteristic avoidance of metaphoric comparisons. As proof, he cites 'Still ruht der See' [Quiet lies the sea], and contrasts its non-metaphoric austerity to the metaphoric outburst of comparisons in one of Wieland's sunsets.

He completely fails to see that Goethe is full of precisely verbal metaphors. The most primal, the very deepest, and therefore, the most sensuously captivating. And least of all objectively visible, more in the muscular system, through the reproduction of trans-visually perceptible metaphors (both 'trans' meaning *vorbei* [along; past], and 'trans' in the sense of *mimisch* [mimic]). Fogs *'schleichen'* [creep], a lake *'ruht'* [rests].

It is this process that Disney palpably and objectively depicts in drawings.

It is not just waves, factually boxing the side of a steamship. (And in accordance with the well-known formula of the comical, therefore, gathering its outlines into a boxing glove).

It is also the amazing, elastic play of the contours of Disney's images.

With surprise—necks elongate.

With panicked running—legs stretch.

With fright—not only the character trembles, but a wavering line runs along the contour of its drawn image.

And it is here in this very link of the drawing, that there is accomplished precisely that, for which we have cited so many examples and excerpts.

Here is a very curious phenomenon.

For if, in terror, the neck of a horse or cow stretches, then the representation itself of the skin will stretch but not the contour of the drawing of the skin as an independent element.

In such stretching of the neck, neither will there be that which we said of the running away road, or the skipping contour of the mountain ridge.

And only after the contour of the neck elongates beyond the possible limits of the neck does it become a comical embodiment of that which occurs as a sensuous process in the cited metaphors.

The comicality here stems from the fact that any representation exists in two ways: as a set of lines, and as the image that arises from them.

The graphic drawing of numerals and hands on a clock face, and an image of the time of day that comes from their specific combination.

Normally, this is indissoluble.

In an affect—this is broken (Vronsky glances at the clock on the veranda of the Karenins' home after Anna has informed him of her pregnancy, and sees only a geometric pattern, not being in a state to comprehend what time it is).

In a comical construction, there is also dissection but of a special type: the perception of them as independent of each other, and simultaneously as belonging together.

That is, a picture, formally and mechanically in stasis, reproducing the *dialectical* idea of the unity of oppositions, in which each by itself opposition at the same time coexists in unity, which is possible only in a process, in movement, in dynamics.

(Compare the snake devouring its own tail in Indian tradition—and the dachshund wrapped around a telegraph pole.)

Upon this principle is constructed Chaplin's wonderful trick in *The Great Dictator*.[86]

On the little barber's store front, Nazi stormtroopers have written the terrible, damning word, 'Jew'. The shell-shocked Chaplin (note the depths of psychological motivations of this comedian) erases this word, taking it for a series of abstract (and devoid of meaning) white streaks.

The comical mechanism is clear. Essence and form are dissected. The effect results from the fact that we know them to be indissoluble and belonging to each other.

The greatness of this comical number, of course, consists of the fact that in its essence racism is nonsense and the comical approach of Chaplin through direct action—in an image of an act—demonstrates this idea materially.

The comicality of the contour of a neck elongating beyond the neck itself, is constructed by Disney upon the same thing and in the same way.

Here, the unity of an object and the form of its representation is dissected.

And the comicality of the effect resides in the fact that their representational co-membership is persistently emphasized. (Take away the representationality of lines. Let them follow the emotions in an abstract, linear, rhythmical and seismographic way—and they'll no longer be comical, but will be the graphic equivalent of Scriabin's colour dreams).[87]

The independently elongating contour is read as a neck going out of itself.

And then it skips over to a comical embodiment of the formula of pathos and ecstasy.

As is well known, this formula consists of the principles of dialectics being taken as the dynamic, compositional source.

And the formula of comical pathos, therefore, is the formula of the most primal comicality.

••

Thus, it turns out that the contour, the outline of a drawing—its generalizing line, suddenly begins to take on an independent life, independent of the figures themselves, the objects themselves.

It is interesting that this seemingly unlikely and inconceivable phenomenon is also connected with definite stages of primitive and primordial thought.

Let us take an example from child psychology—for according to the fundamental biogenetic law, a child not only physically, but also psychically and psychologically, passes through stages which correspond to earlier stages of human development. And the psychology of a child at specific stages of development corresponds to the peculiarities of the psychology of peoples who are the 'childhood stage' of social and societal development.

In looking through Dr Georg Kerschensteiner's impressive research into children's drawings, *The Development of Drawing Skill*,[88] among the many curious peculiarities of children's early drawing, we find the following such case.

It is found in the section devoted to the representation of plants. In Table 61 (p. 199), there is reproduced a drawing by an eight-year-old girl, the daughter of a bricklayer, depicting a tree drawn from memory.

This drawing is remarkable in that within it there exist independently: a line of the general outline of the tree and the system of branches, whose contour in reality, in nature, blends into such an outline. Here, they exist separately, living independently.

The consciousness of the child is not yet capable of comprehending the unity of the whole and part, and the part separately from the whole.

A certain amount of time will pass, and the plastic unity of both will be grasped by the child's eye, just as in the consciousness, there will start to be formed a sense of the unity of the part and the whole.

This moment also occurs in the well-known manner in which children draw a head—as a profile, but sticking both eyes in this profile looking—from a full face position. Here too, the general dimensions of the head and the details of the surface of the face live independent lives, without combining into the realistic unity of a whole image.

••

It is interesting that in the infinite spirals of cultural progress, every time a certain creative cycle finds itself on the threshold of evolution, there occurs an analogous phenomenon with its own qualitative peculiarities.

This usually relates to periods of especial ripeness and impressiveness, characteristic for the primitive stages of a cultural or artistic phenomenon. And especially ripe, precisely because these phenomena, at this stage, structurally reproduce those very same laws, which are characteristic of the structure of primitive and sensuous thought.

Let us recall the two 'ripest' phases in the history of the evolution of theatre: the Italian comedy of masks (*commedia dell'arte*) and the early, pre-Shakespearean dramaturgy of England.

When, in a poetic turn of speech, we fall back on a reconstruction of a similar course of thought, we always come out sensuously enriched. In his tale 'Night'[89] Andersen describes a mother who went after Death to get him to return her dead child. She cried her eyes out, because only at this price could she cross the lake; and so as to be able to penetrate the dwelling-place of Death, she gave up to the old gravedigger 'her long black hair, receiving in exchange—the old woman's grey hair!'

This trait of the 'division of a unity' makes just as strong an impression as its opposite: a forcible merger, especially in those cases when it is not just a flashy, formal trick, but when there truly underlies it not an objective unity, but a much more profound moral, conceptual or thematic unity.

For example, Bierce's staggering description in his story 'Captain Coulter'[90] when the colonel goes down into the cellar of a plantation house and suddenly sees a man with a long, jet-black beard slouched over. The man turns out to be Captain Coulter, who had been forced by the artillery general to fire upon his own house. And what had appeared to be a black beard, turns out to be the dishevelled hair of Coulter's wife, who was killed during the shelling, and whose lips he was kissing in despair.

The effectiveness of this description, of course, comes from the fact that a primitively lowest, sensuous method of exposition fuses together in a formal way that which should exist separately, and it simultaneously serves as a tangible image of the embodiment of Coulter's mad love for his wife, fusing the lovers into a single unit.

A child perceives a verbal picture in precisely the same way. Werner, I believe, cites an example in *Developmental Psychology*[91] of a child who was asked to illustrate with toys the biblical saying: 'Komm, Herr Jesu, sei unser Gast' ['Come, Jesus, be our guest']. The child placed at the table not one figure, but two. When asked who the first one was, he answered: 'Jesus'. The second one turned out to represent . . . the 'guest'. A unity of the invariable and constant ('Jesus') and its temporary, particular aspect (the role of the guest)—does not at all enter the mind and thoughts of a child. The contour of the crown of a tree is not seen as being composed of the countless contours of leaves which make it up. Each one lives separately, independently. Each one trembles on its own, just as the drawing and the contour of Disney's horses, cows, goats, ostriches and monkeys rush along, leaving themselves behind.

In both cases, a single, inviolable characteristicness prevails, namely, a self-contained independence of the outlined character and an independence of his actions.

There is not yet present the element that makes Shakespeare great or any outstanding master of the realistic dramaturgy of later stages.

There is not yet the theory that revelation and formation of personality are determined through action, that an abrupt turning point of action coincides with a revelation of new traits of the human image; that a trait of personality determines the course of action and that an action, in turn, moulds the personality of the character.

In the comedy of masks, there exists a definite set of characters, which remains invariable for the countless number of interludes and comedies, which only in their broadest outlines result from the traditional and once-established pattern of the interaction of the invariable functions of once-established characters, appropriately called not characters, but masks.

These are not the only possible personalities in the only possible connection of dramaturgical events and situations, like Hamlet and Othello; but rather, they are a kaleidoscope of hieroglyphs, complete in themselves, which are combined into any number of patterns of the arbitrary plots of the comedy of masks.

The very same thing is characteristic also of pre-Shakespearean theatre. For Webster[92] too, it is characteristic for the outlining of images and personalities to take place by itself, and the course of situations and events—in its own way, and independently. For here there is the same, almost canonical set of invariable image-masks, such as 'The Revenger', who, only with the arrival of Shakespeare, receives his own paradoxical (for the tradition of the era) reinterpretation in *Hamlet*, but until then, recurs as a finished, traditional stencil throughout a variety of plays and skits, instilling terror in the viewer in exactly the same way that in Italy, through the chain of eternally changing interludes, the figure of 'The Captain' makes him laugh. It is enough to compare his great-great-grandsons—Gautier's 'Captain Fracasse', or Rostand's 'Cyrano de Bergerac',[93] to see clearly the profound connection between the personality of the character and the action of the play, in contrast to the early stage, where the independence of the separate existence of both is invariable.

The very same peripeteias have been experienced by such a popular and unquestionable unity as 'the unity of form and content'.

Outside of the perfection in works of classical completeness, even this seemingly inseparable, organic unity opens up or comes apart.

For periods of changing phases, of mutation of styles, or of definition of new social formations, there takes place an unbalanced outstripping of one by the other.[94]

For periods of collapse, i.e. a regressive return to primitive patterns, there is characteristically the very same collapse of the unity of form and content, as for periods standing on the threshold of their future merger.

Construction becomes an end in itself. Composition—the sole content of the thing. Anecdote—a comprehensive value of a formless work.

IV

[*Alma-Ata, 3 December 1943*]

DISNEY

Bambi, of course, must not be ignored.[95]

Bambi, is already a shift towards ecstasy—serious, eternal: the theme of *Bambi* is the circle of life—*the repeating circles of lives.*

No longer the sophisticated smile of the twentieth century towards totems. But a return to pure totemism and a *Rück-Ruck* [reverse shift] towards evolutionary prehistory.

A humanized deer, or rather, *Rückgänglich* conversely, a 're-deerized' human.

Bambi crowns, of course, the whole study on Disney.

Separately, there is still *Fantasia* as an experiment in the realization of *synthesis* through *syncretism*.[96]

The greatness of Disney, as the purest example of the application of the method of art in its very purest form.

[*Kratovo*], *8 July 1946*

Life arrives (11 March 1946 issue).

Again, an absolutely ingenious, new Disney: *Make Mine Music*.[97]

Traditional and mediocre (in terms of the drawing) is Sergei Prokofiev's *Peter and the Wolf.*

In the same family is *Casey at the Bat.*[98]

But absolutely stunning is *Willie the Operatic Whale*.[99]

A startling juncture in the triangle with two other Americans—Melville (*Moby Dick*) and . . .

Edgar Poe (*The Pit and the Pendulum*).

A trans-oceanic juncture with my *The Terrible*—the murder of Vladimir.

(Strictly, through *Ivan*, I also thus read Willie.)

It begins with an absolutely wild, direct kick, which you receive from the page with the three pictures where Willie performs in the Met (Metropolitan Opera).

The very same kick which is always connected with subconscious mechanisms.

And the kick is very quickly deciphered into the fact that we are dealing here for the first time, perhaps, in Disney (or so clearly, at any rate) with prenatal[100] elements expressed not as a process, but as an object.

Usually Disney (for the most part) appeals to this realm through the structure of his works, through devices, through elements of form.

For example, the 'plasma appeal' in (1) *a varying contour*—expanding necks and legs, or (2) *variations of species*: octopuses—elephants, striped fish—tigers in *Merbabies* (cf. the same thing, but non-comical, for it is comparatively metaphorical, in D. H. Lawrence, when D. H. compares horses with butterflies or fish; for example, in *St Mawr*).[101]

One could call this the protean element, for the myth of Proteus (behind whom there seems to be some especially versatile actor) or more precisely, the appeal of this myth is based, of course, upon the omnipotence of plasma, which contains in liquid form all possibilities of future species and forms.

It is glaringly significant that this most typical thing for Disney occurs also here, entering into the group of basic and most baffling means of influence: 'Willie not only sings, but is capable of singing in any voice range—

tenor, baritone, soprano or contralto, sometimes all of them at once.'

The significance of this element as protean, i.e. an alterable unit, is emphasized also by the fact that Disney uses for this phenomenal trait of Willie, *not a group* of singers of different registers, which is more than possible during the sound recording—but gives him the voice of the singer phenomenon, Nelson Eddy,[102] who sings by himself the whole range of voices from soprano to bass (I heard such singers in music halls in America and Europe).

'Willie is remarkable for his many voices. All of them, from soprano to bass, belong to Nelson Eddy. To sing a duet with himself, Eddy would record one part, then sing the other while the first was played back. For the 400-voice 'Ave Maria' chorus, a special device multiplied 100 times the quartet of Eddy, Eddy, Eddy and Eddy.'

It is interesting that here the variability is inserted not in the animal itself—not in his forms (octopuses become elephants, a neck grows), but in the voice, with the form of its source remaining unaltered.

A new page in the 'history of Disney'.

During the War, Disney emerges from the infantile and pre-human realm towards maturity.

His pictures become utilitarian—*instructionally technical,* thematically mature, progressive. (A sort of De Seversky's aviation book for me.)[103]

One can admire him, but he is losing one's interest. (N.B. This is being written in Alma-Ata and there are also some notes.)

Then there occurs the same transition to grown up—a transition to man formally, with actors and unsuccessfully: *The Three Caballeros.*[104]

Where a real, three-dimensional man on the human level is mechanically merged with the conventional subhumans of Disney's palette.

Trash in its lack of principle.

Fantasia is two-faced: it is good when in the realm of Disney, the grotesque equivalent of music and animated caricatures.

It is bad when serious or dramatic. (From this point of view, *Bambi* is also bad. Cf. *Non-Indifferent Nature* as to how he ought to have handled *Bambi.*)[105]

Make Mine Music evidently intentionally avoids this.

Walt Disney's newest full-length picture, *Make Mine Music*, is a vaudeville show designed for those who were a little overwhelmed by his high-flown *Fantasia*.

The picture's stars remain in the background only as voices (Nelson Eddy, Jerry Colonna, the Andrews Sisters), as shadows (dancers Tania Riobouchinska and David Lichine), or as tootlers (Mr Goodman and his men). To spectators *Make Mine Music* may seem either a new art form or just a collection of good Technicolor cartoons. Not all the acts quite make the grade, but those that do have all the brilliant imagination of the wonderful Walt at his best.[106]

The latter is not surprising, for Walt makes a correct plunge into the sub-human level—an inexhaustible fund of uniquely, irresistibly active images, wonderful and brilliant in their imagination.

(Imagination—both as inventiveness and as imagery).

As we have seen it is this that grows into the very subjects of the images.

Thus, he emerges from the blind alley and dead end where he had been at the beginning of the 1940s.

In terms of form of audio-visual synthesis and the frameworks available to him in this, the grotesque, cartoon solution of the animated film remains for him, of course, a limitation.

A tragic and dramatic resolution of this synthesis is possible only in the realm where I work.

How interesting! He and I both have—Prokofiev.

Two different Prokofievs: the Sergei Sergeyevich of *Peter and the Wolf* (included in *Make Mine Music*), and the Sergei Sergeyevich of the scores of *Alexander Nevsky* and *Ivan the Terrible,* par excellence.

In the realm of music itself, *Peter and the Wolf* does precisely the same thing that the correct Disney does between music and a cartoon:

an ironic synthesis.

Sergei Sergeyevich's instrumental timbres are comically localized throughout representational, concrete realms.

An enumeration at the beginning: a quacking duck, a cat, a bird, a wolf, Peter.

This is exactly what Disney does in his best films with drawing, doing the same thing in relation to music: an abstract correspondence (the only one possible—cf. *The Film Sense*)[107] of sound and drawing—forcibly clothed in concrete forms (which is why it is funny).

Remaining in the realm of structures, we find not an illustrative correspondence between the essences of the musical movement and the movement of the image.

For example, 'Ocean-Sea, Blue Sea'[108]—where the orchestration is like a synthesis of the traits of the sea.

One group plays the depths of the sea,

another, the play of light along the surface,

a third, the boundless width,

a fourth, the blueness.

(N.B. The first two, he himself pointed out to me at an orchestra rehearsal. Three and four, and many others, are easy to detect.)

It is trite when there is one trait, for example, a graphic surf.

And it is a different matter when 'surfness' repeatedly cuts through a many sided and complex image of the sea à la Sergei Sergeyevich.

Here is both the similarity and the difference of our junctures—Disney's and mine in the same audio-visual field.

And here is also the response to Georges Sadoul, who writes:

Eisenstein's *Ivan the Terrible* is a grandiose work. Prokofiev's wonderful music serves as a base to a counter-point of images which are permeated by certain visual forms, repeated as leitmotifs; the film is to ordinary films what opera is to everyday theatre, and Eisenstein's experiments, through wholly different means and with wholly different aesthetic goals, call to mind certain preoccupations of Walt Disney in *Fantasia*.[109]

V

10 January 1942[110]

We are consciously limiting ourselves to three complete analogies in subject-matter and form to Disney:

Lewis Carroll's *Alice.*

Andersen's *Tales.*

La Fontaine's *Fables.*

The analogy of the resurrection of the natural, the animal (not in the sense of beast but of *das Animalische*), as antitheses:

La Fontaine—17th century (H[ippolyte] Taine).

Anders[en]—18th century (Brandes).

Alice—19th century.

Disney—20th century.

(N.B. Rousseau—*Paul et Virginie*—Andersen.[111] Andersen clearly completes the line of this tendency from the end of the 18th century. La Fontaine pioneers it himself in the 17th century.)

Lewis Carroll is the antithesis of industrial positivist England. (Dickens as well.)

They are interesting as they also stand outside the process of staged development.

• •

The amorality of Carroll (pure fantasy).

The semi-morality of Andersen (not always pure fantasy).

The morality of La Fontaine (rational fantasy).

i.e. the percentage of the consciously and deliberately directed element in them varies.

It is quite interesting that Disney is even further from consciousness than perhaps even Carroll is.

That is, the tendency for the prevalence of pre-logic (its deepening and widening) precisely replicates the growth of the opposite tendency:

Descartes—Voltaire—industrial England (Comte)— industrial America.[112]

The degradation into the pre-logical echoes this crescendo of the rational: La F[ontaine], And[ersen], Carroll—Disney.

The crescendo of the purity of the pre-logical method moves in the opposite direction in its striving for the absolute original.

20 November 1943 [113]

Disney has beasts.

Humanized beasts.

Tiens!

The theme of the 'humanization of the ape' is crucial in the history of the evolution of the human race. (Cf. Engels and the role of labour in this.)

And Disney's whole opus is a song about this.

A song about this that is funny.

For the gradual process of unity in development is replaced by the instantaneity of equalization.

And here we have both: the secret of effectiveness as I understand it—the everlasting nature of the subject and the secret of the mechanics of what is funny.

The only thing that is effective is something that in the form of its expression (isn't the humanization of beasts a shell—a form of narrative appropriate to the tasks of the contents that the author sets himself: Goethe in *Reineke*, the Greek in *Batrachomyomachia* or Disney in *Mickey Mouse*)[114] is, in terms of evolution, historical (regressive) and it is funny that the truly dynamic process is replaced by its formal (static) application.

27 November 1943

John Phoenix's *Tuskmaker's Toothfiller* does, of course, stand in line with other plasmatic fancies. Never observed this before. Now I have read Walter de la Mare's rhymes on this subject in *Nonsense Verse* (from *Stuff and Nonsense*, pp. 234–5):

> He laid forthwith poor Mr Smith
> Close-clamped upon the table,
> And, cold as stone, took out his bones
> As fast as he was able.[115]

ALSO:

> The neck (and growth) in *Alice in Wonderland*.[116]
> The long-armed boy of Trier.

Japanese caricatures of necks and arms (p[ar] ex[emple] of the geishas drawing people to Yoshiwara.

Something, of course, even in Grandville's *Un autre monde*.[117] And now these jelly stories.[118]

The human snake in the circus.

Snake dancers in the nightclubs of Harlem.[119]

The formation of a skeleton (internal in man, external in a shellfish).

The ossification of a cartilage (the little temple of a child).

Ontogenetically in terms of evolution.

And the sporadic hardening of tissue in the play of stretched muscle.

The mimicry (*d'après* Michelet: *L'Oiseau, L'Insecte*) from static mask-faces of a fly and a snake to mobile features.

A[lma-]Ata. The mountains. The Sanatorium.
2 December 1943

As usual. It is enough, when choking with delight, to read
something, as it turns out that these things invariably fit
into the research material.

This is understandable. For me objects of a quite precise stamp are thrilling. And they interest me in terms of
research.

It is however pleasant that this kind of stuff usually
comes to me *par l'amour.* That gives it a certain suavity,
vigour, emphasizing, instead do academic aridity.

Something useful, not to say—boyish.

Anyhow, I am enraptured by D. H. Lawrence's *St
Mawr.*[120]

So then I am enraptured by *St Mawr,* this hymn to the
Great God Pan, who has now become no more than the
Great Goat Pun (*je cité l'auteur:*[121] *the pun about Pan may
not be of too high a class—but fitting its purpose*).

Somewhere in the background memory lures.

Agniya. The Proletkult period. *Wise Man.*[122]

Horseback riding for all of us.

Agniya. With this Dostoyevsky name.

Agniya—the first I slept with.

Agniya weaving into one pattern:

Arvatov, Vertoff, myself and a big, big white stallion.[123] (In the stable on Granatny Lane.)

I have forgotten the name of this enormous white stallion.

He and Vertov served to arouse my jealousy.[124]

The *intimité* between Agniya and the (white) stallion was blindingly obvious.

The rival tried to draw in her little hand with his hot lips. (Strangely, I cannot recall—and it is all the same to me—whether her hand was small.)

Arvatov went out of his mind.

Basically, because of me.

The stallion had nothing to do with it. Many years later.

This is what Fate wanted.

Agniya is living (lived) alone in one house—a wing of the Herzen House[125] with Madame.[126]

Married to some kind of national.[127]

A slant-eyed child with high cheek bones.

She became friendly with Madame naturally because of me.

The white stallion was good.

Poor Arvatov.

Agniya poisoned herself.

I left with Verka Yanukova.[128]

However, none of this, apart from the stallion, has any relevance.

St Mawr will be a chapter in my *Disney!*

Lawrence's epic is totemically bestial. Domesticated and longing (evidently, still—the peace par excellence) as counterpart to Lautréamont and his actively sadistic epic of a beast as opposed to Lawrence's passive moan.[129]

A noter beyond this:

The stallion and fire.

There is an extremely interesting path of metaphors not merely of man through beast (and vice versa) but also of beast through beast (is this its strange humanization?): St Mawr jumps like a fish and sits, legs spread wide like a lizard. Horses skim over the fields like playing . . . butterflies (*à noter*: Lou and Rico's marriage is compared to a similar play of butterflies—N.B. Entirely irrespective of and quite disconnected from this image.)

This recalls Disney's *Merbabies*[130] with its metamorphosis of the animals into one another. The elephant family from a group of octopuses, the fish-tiger in the cage, circus riding on sea-horses, and so on.

And, of course, the downfall into another world of the beginning—carrying the young children down a *spiral* into the underwater depths.

Compare Alice and the fall through a Rabbit Hole. The White Rabbit—Dean So and So, incorporated by Carroll into his person, see *Slang Today and Yesterday*.[139]

This downfall of the worlds through the eyes of St Mawr and the numerous generations of the gradual domestication of animals.

The juncture between Disney's theme (*au comique*) of the humanization of beasts (as I noticed a couple of days ago) and the domestication of a man (in Lawrence).

Lawrence and Lautréamont as semi-tragic and tragic counterparts of Disney?

Of course, the whole of Lawrence's opus is *animalisé*.

Cf. the collection of his verses about animals—an unsurpassed depiction of them.

The examples are usually metaphorical as well. Thus, Donald (in *Women in Love*) is everywhere compared to a stallion (of the St Mawr type), and some kind of lady is marvellously linked to a cat.

Here we may take a side glance at Balzac. (*Un Amour dans le désert*), where this is simply a stage reverse metaphor *avant tout*: see the descriptions and comparisons of the tigress and the lioness of the demi-monde. (Anyhow fits in quite nicely.)

Deal with extracts of the most striking passages from *St Mawr*.

The theme of the vampire is charmingly handled in *The Lovely Lady* using all the tricks of modern psychology—the Oedipus [complex], and so on.

3 December 1943

Why the horse is called St Mawr I do not know. However, everything that concerns manly sensuality if for Lawrence apparently determined by a Moor [*mavr*]. Hence, in *The Lovely Lady* Aunt Pauline's lover, the Jesuit priest (the father of her second son Robert) who incorporates the masculine principal—bears the name of Mauro: 'No, Robert dear, you will never be the man your father was,' this miraculously preserved 72-year-old vampire-woman whispered to herself in a monologue overheard by her niece through a water pipe from the roof. 'Though you have some of his looks. He was a marvellous lover, soft as a flower yet piercing likea humming-bird. No, Robert dear, you will never know how to serve a woman as Monsignor Mauro did. *Caro, caro mio bellissimo, it ho aspettato como l'aggonizzante aspetta la morte, morte deliziosa, quasi quasi troppo deliziosa per un'anima umana*—soft as a flower, yet probing like a humming-bird. He gave himself to a woman as he gave himself to God. Mauro, Mauro. How you loved me.'

...MOOR...

As the background to primitive passions (England, my England).

In this respect the tradition of *Wuthering Heights* by Miss Brontë.

St Mawr is for all that about a horse (and allegorically not about it but about a human, or to be even more precise here, about a man) as is *Kholstomer*.[132]

It would be interesting to compare them.

The most interesting thing, however, is that in Tolstoy an animal is placed on the same level as a primitively, spontaneously, thinking person, whereas in Lawrence, animals stand beyond the boundaries of the human in the elementary spontaneity of their existence.

In Tolstoy, they are domesticated, servants of natural morality, in Lawrence a proud, wild embodiment of the primitive instinct for life as the foundations for the highest superhuman morality, potential and strength—higher than any catechizes.

N.B. Cf. *Metzengerstein* and the animals in Poe.

Shift and movement in Shakespeare's linguistic forms according to Spurgeon.[133] On metamorphoses in Shakespeare.

A[LMA-] A[TA]
5 January 1944

Disney *in totem*.

In plastic terms Mickey effectively embodies the ideals of the Bororo—he is both a human and a mouse!

(And N.B. Inescapably comic! Because his unity is not dynamic.)

GRUNDPROBLEM, A[LMA-]A[TA]
2 June 1944

On the self-portrait in my scheme in connection with Disney.

In my scheme, what is also very good is the model of an initial bifurcation of two tendencies—self-embodiment and the embodiment of the objective worlds in each work.

If the top is Zola's formula '*Une réalité vue à travers un tempérament*' [a reality viewed through a temperament], then down below, there is a similar separate but parallel existence between *réalité* and *temperament*—the 'I' in Peruvian plastic art on the waters and in Grecian perspectives. Here the water, in self-portrait terms, is an objectively reflecting drawing.

The fact of the water does not yet infuse the reflected image of reality. It *existe côte à côte* [exists alongside].

In literature, this stage consists in the collective 'graft'—the forerunner of the refrain, i.e. of the emotional intonation taken beyond the bounds of the narrative part into the rudiments of a future refrain (at the end or beginning).

All these 'oi did lado', 'la-ri-ri' etc—are of course the same as the pot beneath the figure in Peruvian plastic art.

Thereupon, it grows into a refrain.

But further the intonation , i.e. the individual-emotional—plunges into the tall[134] refrain construction, for instance Yvette Guilbert's *St Nicolas*:[135] an objective narrative in a couplet and an abruptly changing emotional commentary in the performance of the refrain. This is so wonderfully effective, it is so . . . immortal, because it is the reconstructed history of coming into being, the stage of this history of coming into being, of the later *uns über-bürdiges* [burdensome to us] forms.

Here one of the most profound attractions of the rudimentarily psychological [principles] besides the pure rhythmic system—is pleasure in the diversity of refrain (great).

The same is true of Mickey as a self-portrait of Disney, where the gestural self-embodiment (as base for each embodiment) is still gesturally figurative (and that's why , funny). The embodiment is also in the animals, i.e the whole chain of incarnations from Jupiter to Kipling (*Mowgli*).

2 June 1944

Emphasize the importance of the fact that Mickey is a self portraiture of Disney.

Here a digression on self portraiture as the first stage of the embodiment of the objective world—not yet separated from the subjective world—in pottery primitive, and in Grecian and Peruvian show that in them right the way through the subjective (*le pot*) and the objective (the drawn or plastic figures upon the pot) are already being separately represented, precisely because, probably, of the style of high objectivity (Peru).

NOTES

1 Walt Disney (1901–66) was the leading commercial animator in American cinema and E met him when he went to Hollywood in 1930. Beginning with *Steamboat Willie* [1928], the Walt Disney Studio produced 121 Mickey Mouse shorts. The figure of 52 a year cited by E is clearly exaggerated.

2 *The Skeleton Dance* [1928] was the first cartoon in the Silly Symphony series, directed by Walt Disney. In this series the animated screen action was created specifically to match the rhythm of the pre-recorded music track, rather than vice versa, as had previously been the custom.

3 Fra Angelico (Guido di Pietro, *c.*1400–55), Florentine painter known for the delicate colour of his frescoes.

4 Hans Christian Andersen (1805–75), Danish author of fairy tales and fables.

   Alice's Adventures in Wonderland [1865] was the first children's book written by Lewis Carroll (Charles Dodgson, 1832–98).

5 Ernst Theodor Amadeus Hoffmann (1776–1822) was one of the leading writers of German Romanticism.

6 Lindhorst was an acquaintance of Hoffmann and the butt of many jokes and fantastic stories amongst his circle of friends. Hoffmann gave the name to the hero of his play *Der goldne Topf* ['The Golden Pot' or 'The Golden Flower Pot', 1814]. See E. T. A. Hoffmann, *The Selected Writings of E. T. A. Hoffmann* (L. J. Kent & E. C. Knight ed. and trans.) (Chicago: University of Chicago Press, 1969).

7 *Merbabies* [1938] was a Silly Symphony directed by George Stallings.

8 The manuscript contains the following notation in parentheses: 'O. Henry and city slums.' O. Henry (pseudonym of William Sidney Porter, 1862–1910) was an American short-story writer. We may assume that, if E had developed the planned comparison of Disney's films with O. Henry's stories (with their inevitable 'happy endings'), he would have mentioned Lev Kuleshov's film *The Great Consoler* [*Velikii uteshitel*, 1933], which was structured on a counterpoint of three lines: the filming of O. Henry's story, 'A Retrieved Reformation', a depiction of the tragic, real-life fate in gaol of Jimmy Valentine—the 'inmate of the slums', and the perception of 'consoling art' by the poor shop girl, Dulcey. It is apparently in reference to this unwritten passage that E later calls Disney's cinema 'the great consoler'.

9 *The Three Little Pigs* [1933], a *Silly Symphony* directed by Burt Gillett, was awarded a special prize by the jury—chaired by E—at the 1935 Moscow International Film Festival. E further expressed his admiration for the film later in the year when, in response to a film

journal's poll, he cited it as the year's major achievement in the advancement of film art.

10 A note in the manuscript: 'A peu près ainsi. [Something like this.] Only less emotionally.'

11 Walt Whitman (1819–92), American poet.

12 A suburb in the south-west of Moscow where E's dacha was located.

13 *Snow White and the Seven Dwarfs* [1937] was Disney's first feature-length cartoon film and was a major box-office success.

14 The 'Dry Law' is a reference to the 18th Amendment to the US Constitution, which came into effect on 16 January 1920 and prohibited the manufacture, sale or transportation of alcohol. That power was returned to the states by the 21st Amendment, ratified on 5 December 1933.

15 On a separate page E made this note: 'In Chapter Five, however, poor Alice again experiences the same adventures. Here, the sides of a mushroom have the same magical effect.' He then cites the corresponding passage in a Russian translation made by himself, as were all the other citations from the Lewis Carroll story.

16 Walter Trier (1890–1951) was a German cartoonist and illustrator of children's novels by Erich Kästner (1899–1974): *Emil and the Detectives* [1929] and *Arthur with the Long Arm* [1931], which E is referring to here.

17 Yoshiwara was the pleasure district of Edo (modern Tokyo), catering for the merchant class from the 18th century. Its inhabitants were courtesans and Kabuki theatre actors and these were celebrated in the woodcuts of various Japanese artists of the time. See

also *ESW4*, pp. 224–5 and: C. S. Seigle, Yoshiwara, *The Glittering World of the Japanese Courtesan* (Honolulu: University of Hawaii Press, 1993); J. E. De Becker, *Nightless City of Geisha: The History of the Yoshiwara* (London: Kegan Paul, 2002).

18 Honoré de Balzac (1799–1850) was the French author of a cycle of over eighty novels to which he gave the generic title 'La Comédie humaine' [The Human Comedy].

19 The section enclosed in square brackets which follows this paragraph was written on 6 October 1940 and is marked: 'Between plasmation and fire'. This later insertion replaced the following sentences of the first-draft text: 'But there is yet another element, even more plasmatic, more free in its diversity, more tempestuous in the rate at which it engenders the most unexpected outlines. And, of course, it to is rendered its due by Disney's creative imagination. *The Moth and the Flame* is the name of this film.'

20 *Lonesome Ghosts* [1937], a Mickey Mouse film directed by Burt Gillett.

21 The title characters of a comic strip by the German cartoonist, Wilhelm Busch (1832–1908). An English translation appears in: W. Arndt (ed.), *The Genius of Wilhelm Busch: Comedy of Frustration* (Los Angeles: University of California Press, 1982).

22 The manuscript contains the following marginal note: 'Modern Times'. E undoubtedly intended to mention Chaplin's *Modern Times* [USA, 1936], which contains a satirical scene of a conveyor-belt system that turns man into an appendage of machinery, a device that had

previously been used (although not satirically) in Fritz Lang's *Metropolis* [Germany, 1927].

23 Reference to *Self Control* [1938], a Donald Duck short directed by Jack King.

24 Mary Baker Eddy (1821–1910) was an American religious leader and founder of the Christian Science movement. Aimee Semple McPherson (1899–1944) was an American evangelist and faith healer.

25 *Hawaiian Holiday* [1937], a Mickey Mouse film directed by Ben Sharpsteen.

26 *The Moth and the Flame* [1938], a *Silly Symphony* directed by Burt Gillett.

27 Erich Wulffen (1862–1936), author of *Der Sexualverbrecher: ein Handbuch für Juristen* [The Sexual Criminal. A Handbook for the Judiciary], 11th EDN (Hamburg: Langenscheidt, 1928). E's copy is dated 20 September 1940.

28 Iwan Bloch (1872–1922), German psychologist whose work, *Beiträge zur Aetiologie der Psychopathia Sexualis* [Essays on the Aetiology of Psychopathia Sexualis] (Berlin: n.p., 1903), is cited by Wulffen.

39 Paul Adolf Näcke (1851–1913), German psychologist, author of 'Feuermanie' [Pyromania] in the *Hans Gross Archiv für Kriminal-Anthropologie und Kriminalistik* [Hans Gross Archive for Criminal Anthropology and Criminology], VOL. 26 (Leipzig: Verlag von F. C. W. Vogel, 1912), cited by Wulffen.

30 A note in the manuscript: 'Hempelmann'. The reference is to Friedrich Albert Hempelmann (1878–1954), a German zoopsychologist highly regarded by E and whose book *Tierpsychologie vom Standpunkte des Biolo-*

gen [Animal Psychology from the Standpoint of a Biologist] (Leipzig: Akademische Verlagsgesellschaft, 1926) E repeatedly cited in his writings.

31 E had produced Wagner's opera at the Bolshoi Theatre, Moscow, in 1940. He discusses his approach to directing the opera, in particular the 'Feuerzauber' episode, in 'The Incarnation of Myth', *ESW3*, pp. 142–69; see also *FEL*, pp. 84–91.

32 Rachilde was the pseudonym of Marguérite Vallette Eymery (1860–1953), a French writer closely associated with the Symbolists, whose novel Les Hors-Nature was first published in Paris in 1897.

33 (E's note) Cf. Charles Francis Potter, *The Story of Religion* (New York: Grosset & Dunlap, 1929).

34 (E's note) In *Snow White*, the Wicked Queen stares into fire, and a face of fire prophesies to her about Snow White!

35 This sentence was left unfinished in the manuscript. E possibly had in mind Napoleon's story 'The Mask of the Prophet'. In the culmination of this story the hero, Hakem, having led a revolt against the Caliph and suffered defeat, burns the bodies of his soldiers in a gigantic fire, and then himself. See: C. Frayling (ed.), *Napoleon Wrote Fiction* (Salisbury: Compton Press, 1972).

36 Maxim Gorky (pseudonym of Alexei M. Peshkov, 1868–1936), Russian Realist writer and playwright. The reference is to: Maxim Gorky, 'Fires' in *Fragments from My Diary* (M. Budberg trans.) (New York: Praeger, 1972). All excerpts from Gorky in the present publication are from this edition, modified occasionally

by Alan Upchurch to conform more closely to the original Russian text.

37 Stéphane Mallarmé (1842–98), French Symbolist poet.

38 Following this paragraph there is a gap in the manuscript and a note: 'Hamlet and clouds'. E undoubtedly intended to include here his interpretation of the dialogue between Hamlet and Polonius about the shape of a cloud (*Hamlet*, III.2). He later used the same example in *Nonindifferent Nature*, (*IP3*, pp. 365–6, here based on Alan Upchurch's translation; cf. *NIN*, pp. 330–1):

> This point in the tragedy has been given countless different interpretations based on the reasoning that the cloud preserves its outlines, and the Prince arbitrarily changes his interpretation of its contours. The scene is therefore usually discussed as Hamlet's mockery of Polonius or as a continuation by the Danish Prince of the game of madness. I don't think this is quite correct, and above all because in reality no-one pictures to himself the outlines of a cloud in the way that is described here. And furthermore the succession of contours of a camel, [a weasel] and a whale are completely logical successive phases of a cloud changing its form . . . Therefore, it seems to me that the three successive comparisons represent above all the passage of time— the time in which the cloud twice manages to alter its form.

39 Ivan A. Krylov (1769–1844), sometimes known as the 'Russian La Fontaine', was the author of classic Russian fairy tales.

40 Following this paragraph there is a gap in the manuscript and a note: 'Zola (La Débâcle). The Tuileries fire'. We have filled in this gap with the text in square brackets, a fragment from *Nonindifferent Nature* (*NIN*) in which E cites the same excerpt in a different context; cf. *NIN*, p. 77.

41 This translation, from Part III, is taken from Leonard Tancock's translation, *The Debacle* (Harmondsworth: Penguin, 1972), pp. 489–92.

42 *Sudebnaia psikhiatriia*, (Moscow: Iuridicheskoe izdatel'stvo NKIu SSSR, 1941), p. 160.

43 This translation by R. Dixon is taken from: *The Holy Family, or Critique of Critical Critique* (Moscow: Foreign Languages Publishing House, 1956), p. 168.

44 Jean de La Fontaine (1621–95), French poet and fable writer.

45 Hippolyte Adolphe Taine (1828–93), *La Fontaine et ses fables*, 24th EDN (Paris: H. Fournier, n.d)., pp. 162–5.

46 Ibid., p. 179.

47 E's reference: *Der alte Chinese Tschuang-Tse. Deutsche Auswahl von Martin Buber* (Leipzig: Insel Verlag, 1910). This English translation by Burton Watson is taken from: Chuang Tzu, *Basic Writings* (New York: Columbia University Press, 1964), p. 110.

48 Grandville was the pseudonym of Jean Ignace Isidore Gérard (1803–47), French caricaturist, illustrator and satirist. E especially admired his book, Un Autre

monde, Paris: H. Fournier, 1844, to which he here refers.

49 Taine, p. 167.

50 Jean Pierre Claris de Florian (1755–94), French dramatist, novelist and fable writer.

51 E's manuscript contains a note: 'Gold Rush', a reference to the famous 'dance of the rolls' scene in Chaplin's 1925 film.

52 Georges Louis Leclerc de Buffon (1707–88), French naturalist and author of the 36-volume *Histoire naturelle* (1749–88).

53 Taine, *La Fontaine*, pp. 207–8.

54 The 1940 text ends here with the note: '(Citation). Metamorphosis into Metamorphoses'. The citation from Ovid's *Metamorphoses* was not however included. Judging from the first draft materials and notes, it is apparent that E was planning to draw yet another analogy to Disney's work—the tales of Hans Christian Andersen, based on an analysis made of them in an article by the outstanding Danish literary critic, Georg Brandes (1842–1927). The text that follows in square brackets is a note made by E two years later.

55 *Paul et Virginie* was a sentimental novel published in 1787 by Bernardin de Saint-Pierre.

56 (E's note) Doubly animated: both in the sense of the animated immobility of a drawing, and in the sense of animals, animated with human traits and emotions. Animated both 'physically' and 'spiritually'!

57 The Batrachomyomachia (literally 'the battle of the frogs and mice') was an early Greek poem parodying the epic style and subject of the Iliad.

58 Probably a reference to: E. Nevill Jackson, *The History of Silhouettes* (London: The Connoisseur, 1911), which E owned a copy of.

59 E. Sydow, 'Die Kunst der Naturvölker und der Vorzeit' [The Art of Native Peoples and Prehistoric Times] in *Propyläen-Kunstgeschichte*, VOL. 1 (Berlin: Propyläen-Verlag, 1923).

60 The following note, written by E on 14 October 1944, may help to explain this sentence:

> Here magic is not just an empty phrase of speech. For art (true art) artificially returns the viewer to the stage of sensuous thought—its norms and conditions—which is also the stage of a magical relationship with nature. When you achieve, for example, a synaesthetic blending of sound and image—you have subjected the viewer's perception to the conditions of sensuous thought, where synaesthetic perception is the only kind possible —there is not yet any differentiation of perceptions. And your viewer is 'rebuilt' in accordance with the norms not of the present, but those of primordially sensuous perception—he is 'returned' to the conditions of the magical stage of experiencing the world. And an Idea, carried by means of such a system of influence, given form through such means— irresistibly controls emotion. For the senses and consciousness in such a condition are subjugated and controlled almost as if in a trance. And, because of the passively magical state of the perceiver, art is simultaneously actively

magical in terms of influence and control over the viewer by the artist-magician.

61 To this passage E appended the following citation from *Webster's Dictionary*:

> Animal . . . —Lat. Anima—breath, soul . . . akin to Lat. Animus—soul, mind. Greek anemos—breath, wind. Sanskrit an to breathe, to live. . . To supply with life, to enliven; as how the soul animates the body . . . An animated picture. Animism—from Lat. Anima: soul . . . The belief that all objects possess a natural life or vital force or that they are endowed with an indwelling spirit. The term is usually used to designate the most primitive and superstitious forms of religion.

62 E. G. Kagarov, 'Tipicheskoe razvitie religiozno-mifo-logicheskago tvorchestva' [The Typical Development of Religio-Mythological Creativity], *Voprosy teorii i psikhologii tvorchestva* [Problems in the Theory and Psychology of Creativity], VOL. 5 (Moscow: Kharkov, 1914), pp. 374–5.

63 Reference to the Soviet linguist Nikolai Ya. Marr (1864–1934) who theorized that all words denoting 'birds' and 'sky' in ancient and primitive languages derive from the same prehistoric root, which arose when primitive man did not yet differentiate between the two concepts. For a discussion of Marr's theories and his debt to Lévy-Bruhl, see: L. L. Thomas, *The Linguistic Theories of N. Ja. Marr* (Berkeley: University of California Press, 1957).

64 E. B. Tyler, *Primitive Culture*, VOL. 2, 4th EDN (New York: Brentano's, 1924), pp. 281, 285. E cites from the

Russian edition: *Pervobytnaia kul'tura* (Moscow: Sotsekiz, 1939).

65 Cited in: Tyler, *Primitive Culture*, p. 281.

66 (E's note) 'Self-denying'—the basic mark of ecstatic immersion.

67 (E's note) 'Play'—variability.

68 (E's note) 'Music'—the element of Disney.

69 Lenin, *Philosophical Notebooks*, p. 263.

70 Reference to Engels' 'Landschafte' [1840], translated in: K. Marx & F. Engels, *Collected Works*, VOL. 2 (London: Lawrence & Wishart, 1975). E discusses this work in detail in: *NIN*, pp. 376–8.

71 Translated as 'The Structure of the Film' in *FiFo*, pp. 150–78; and as 'On the Structure of Things' in: *NIN*, pp. 3–37.

72 Reference to the Russian philologist Alexander N. Veselovsky (1838–1906), whose 1898 article, 'Psikhologicheskii parallelism i ego formy v otrazhenii poeticheskago stil'ia' [Psychological Parallelism and Its Forms Reflected in Poetic Style], E quotes from *Istoricheskaia poetika* [Historical Poetics] (Leningrad: GIKhL, 1940). For a discussion of Veselovsky's place in Russian letters and his influence on later writers, see: V. Erlich, *Russian Formalism: History—Doctrine*, 3rd EDN (New Haven, CT: Yale University Press, 1981).

73 Lucien Lévy-Bruhl (1857–1939), French anthropologist whose theoretical views and observations exerted a strong influence on E. In his book, Les Fonctions mentales dans les sociétés inférieures, Lévy-Bruhl cites the evidence of Carl Lumholtz concerning the concepts of the Huichol Indian tribe: ' "Corn, deer and

hikuli" (a sacred plant) are, in a way, one and the same thing to the Huichol.' (C. Lumholtz, Symbolism of the Huichol Indians, p. 22). At first this identification seems absolutely inexplicable. To make it intelligible, Lumholtz explains it on utilitarian grounds: 'Corn is deer (food substance) and hikuli is deer (food substance) and corn is hikuli . . . all being considered identical in so far as they are food substances. Lévy-Bruhl interprets this fact from the point of view of his own concept of participation (see note below): 'in these collective representations of the Huichols . . . the hikuli, deer and corn participate in mystic qualities of the highest importance to the tribe and, for this reason, are considered as "the same thing"' [Lévy-Bruhl, *How Natives Think* (L. A. Clare trans.) (New York: Alfred A. Knopf, 1926), pp. 122–3].

74 Next to this heading in the manuscript E made the following note: 'F and C' (i.e. 'Form and Content'). In *Method*, E substantiates in detail 'form as a stage of content' of an artistic work. The correlations between the categories of form and content in E's aesthetic system are discussed in his article 'Perspectives' (*ESW1*, pp. 138–50, *FEL*, pp. 35–47).

75 In *Method*, E explains that ancient (in particular, ancient Indian) concepts of the 'migration of souls' were a 'presentiment of evolutionary theories' which later found scientific expression in Charles Darwin's *The Origin of Species*.

76 This fragment is taken from E's speech to the January 1935 conference (*ESW3*, p. 32; cf. 'Film Form: New Problems', *FiFo*, pp. 135–6), and fills a gap left in the manuscript with the note: 'Bororo and parrots'. In the

archive there also exists this note dated 5 January 1944:
'Mickey plastically truly embodies the "ideals of the
Bororo"—he is both human and a mouse! (And—N.B.
—unavoidably comical! For this unity is not dynamic.)'

77 The manuscript contains this note: 'Examples in
Veselovsky, *Istoricheskaia poetika*, pp. 522–4. To be
copied out later.'

78 (E's reference) *Istoricheskaia poetika* [1940], pp. 192–3

79 (E's reference) *Istoricheskaia poetika* [1940], p. 524.

80 (E's reference) *Istoricheskaia poetika* [1940], p. 125.

81 In his copy of *Les Fonctions mentales dans les sociétés
inférieurs*, E marked the following assertions of Lévy-
Bruhl:

> In his recent work on Animism in the Indian
> [i.e. Indonesian—R.T.] Archipelago, Kruijt
> believes it necessary to distinguish two suc-
> cessive stages in the evolution of primitive
> communities: one in which individual spirits
> are reputed to inform and inspire every being
> and every object (animals, plants, boulders,
> stars, weapons, tools, and so forth), and
> another and earlier one, in which individual-
> ization has not yet taken place, in which there
> is a diffused principle capable of penetrating
> everywhere, a kind of universal and wide-
> spread force which seems to animate persons
> and things, to act in them and endow them
> with life. (Kruijt, *Het animisme in den indischen
> archipel*, 1906, pp. 66–7.) ... The differentia-
> tion of these two periods corresponds to a dif-
> ference in the mentality of the social group.

At the time when souls are not yet individualized, the individual consciousness of every member of the group is and remains strictly solidary with the collective consciousness. It does not distinctly break away from it; it does not even contradict itself in uniting with it; that which does dominate it is the uninterrupted feeling of participation. Only later, when the human individual becomes clearly conscious of himself as an individual, when he explicitly differentiates himself from the group of which he feels himself a member, do beings and objects outside himself also begin to appear to him as provided with individual minds or spirits during this life and after death. (*How Natives Think*, p. 365)

E made the following note in the margins of the book: 'A bit more complex and not so direct: this does not define "animism", but merely why there are gradations in its evolution; cf. my writings.' E's understanding of this problem, which plays an important role in his article on Disney, was set out in a note he wrote on 3 March 1933 and inserted into Lévy-Bruhl's book:

Animism is quite clearly no more and no less than a transitional stage between pre-logical and logical thought in the part of it that concerns the unity of subject and object. At first 'I' and an object are one. Then there arises the element: both one and not one, but still without a qualitative differentiation between the attributes of 'I' and the object: the object continues to be regarded as independent of the 'I', but not independent of the attributes of the 'I'; i.e. the same thing is considered to be present in it that you start to notice about yourself (hunger, emotions, etc.) A conception of the object is created 'in one' sown image and likeness'—as if a swarm of Regungen [feelings] make sup a soul, the concept of a soul, then objects are endowed with a soul. The point, essentially, is not in a soul, but in the fact that an object is considered to be capable of the same actions as man himself. Then there occurs a second separation —not just from himself, but also from the attributes characteristic of him and by experience not appearing in the object. Thus he enters the stage of contradictions—the basis of logic. *Pour en retourner* [So as to return] to a dialectical unity at the dialectical stage of thought.

82 (E's note) *Istoricheskaia poetika* [1940], p. 126.

83 (E's source reference) In the journal *Teatr* [Theatre] 10 (October 1940). (Editor's note) Translated in: *ESW3*, pp. 142–69, and in a shortened version (which excludes this extract) as 'The Embodiment of a Myth' in: *FEL*, pp. 84–91.

84 (E's note) *Istoricheskaia poetika* [1940], p. 127.

85 Houston Stewart Chamberlain (1855–1927), British-born political philosopher whose racial views were most influential in Germany. He became a German citizen in 1916. E's heavily marked copy of Chamberlain's *Goethe* (Munich: F. Bruckmann, 1912) is dated 8 October 1937.

86 *The Great Dictator* [USA, 1940]. E also discusses this film in his wartime article 'Charlie the Kid', translated in: *ESW3*, pp. 243–67, especially pp. 265–7; cf. *FEL*, pp. 108–39.

87 (E's note) A wonderful, graphic equivalent of exclaiming is the exclamation mark, although it is not funny. But a man who bends over like a question mark, does produce a comical impression. (The situation is not changed by the fact that the origin of the question mark is non-affective, non-gestural.)

Alexander N. Scriabin (also Skriabin, 1872–1915), Russian composer and mystic, whose 1913 'Poem of Fire' (or 'Prometheus') attempted to use light and colour to accompany the musical score.

88 Georg Michael Anton Kerschensteiner (1854–1932), *Die Entwickelung der Zeichnerischen Begabung* (Munich: Carl Gerber, 1905). E refers to the 1914 Russian edition: *Razvitie khudozhestvennogo tvorchestva rebenka* [The Development of a Child's Artistic Creativity].

89 This tale is also known as 'The Story of a Mother'. See: Hans Christian Andersen, *Eighty Fairy Tales* (R. P. Kegwin trans.) (New York: Pantheon Books, 1983).

90 Ambrose Bierce (1842–1914), American humorist and one of E's favourite authors. See also: *ESW3*, p. 262; *ESW4*, pp. 370–2. Here E has in mind 'The Affair at Coulter's Notch', which he analysed in lectures to his class on direction at VGIK on 11 and 18 September 1941. These lectures are translated as *The Short-Fiction Scenario*, also available from Seagull Books.

91 Heinz Werner (1890–1964), author of *Einführung in die Entwicklungspsychologie* [Introduction to Developmental Psychology] (Leipzig: J. A. Barth, 1926). E's

heavily marked copy is dated 26 January 1934. An English translation appeared as *Comparative Psychology of Mental Development* (E. B. Garside trans.) (New York: Harper, 1940).

92 John Webster (*c*.1580–1634), English playwright. *The Revenger's Tragedy* [1607] was not however written by Webster. It was originally attributed to Cyril Tourneur (*c*.1575–1626) but has more recently been assigned to Thomas Middleton (*c*.1580–1627).

93 Théophile Gautier (1811–72), French poet, novelist, and drama and ballet critic. His novel *Le Capitaine Fracasse* was published in 1863. Edmond Rostand (1868–1918), French playwright, whose best known work is *Cyrano de Bergerac* [1897].

94 (E's note) Engels writes about this.

95 *Bambi* [1942], animated feature film.

96 *Fantasia* [1940], feature film that synchronized images to classical music.

97 *Make Mine Music*, feature film produced by Disney in 1946.

98 *Casey at the Bat* [1946], directed by Jack Kinney and produced by Disney, was an animated short based on the classic baseball poem.

199 *Willie the Operatic Whale* [1946], directed by Clyde Geronimi and Hamilton Luske and produced by Disney, was a 15-minute animated short involving, in an alternative title, *The Whale Who Wanted to Sing at the Met*.

100 In the last years of his life E devoted considerable attention to the problems of 'prenatal' or 'intrauterine' memory, believing that this type of memory, formed at

the stage of 'pre-individual existence', plays an enormous role in the unconscious. His hypotheses are expounded in portions of *Method*, and also in his memoirs on which he was also working in 1946.

101 David Herbert Lawrence (1885–1930), English writer. His novella *St Mawr* [1925], set in Shropshire, uses a bay stallion as a symbol of life, beauty, power and passion.

102 Nelson Eddy (1901–67), American baritone and film star.

103 Reference to Alexander De Seversky's bestseller, *Victory though Air Power* (New York: Simon & Schuster, 1942), from which the Disney Studio made a training film with the same title for the US armed forces in 1943.

104 *The Three Caballeros*, a feature film produced by Disney in 1945.

105 E's rather stringent criticisms of *Bambi* are to be found translated in: *NIN*, pp. 389–91.

106 E is here quoting from the review in *Life* (11 March 1946).

107 Reference to the fourth chapter, 'Form and Content: Practice' in *FS*, pp. 157–216. Also translated as the third section of 'Vertical Montage' in *ESW2*, pp. 370–99.

108 Reference to a song written for the 'childhood' prologue to *Ivan the Terrible: Part One*, dropped when E shortened the sequence and moved it from Part One to Part Two as a flashback. See: Y. Tsivian, *Ivan the Terrible* (London: BFI, 2002).

109 (E's note) France–USSR, Numéro spécial: 'Le Cinema soviétique', 1er Avril, 1946.

110 These notes on Disney (RGALI, 1923/2/321–3) supplement those translated by Alan Upchurch in this volume and were first published in this form as 'Zametki ob iskusstve Uolta Disneia' [Notes on the Art of Walt Disney], *Kinovedcheskie zapiski* 52 (2001): 98–115. The translation is by Richard Taylor and annotation draws upon the Russian edition. Parts of the original were written in English, and this has been left as it was.

111 Jean-Jacques Rousseau (1712–78), French political philosopher and inspiration for the Romantic movement. His main work, *The Social Contract*, begins: 'Man is born free and everywhere he is in chains.'

112 René Descartes (1596–1650), Voltaire (1694–1778) and Auguste Comte (1798–1857) were French rationalist philosophers whose ideas underlay the development of industrial society from the 19th century.

113 In the Russian publication, the dates of this note and the next were reversed. I have assumed that this was typographical error and that the notes were printed in chronological order.

114 E is here referring to the satirical verse tale: Johann Wolfgang von Goethe (1749–1832), *Reineke Fuchs* (Reineke Fox), 1793.

115 This is the third stanza of 'Bones', included in the original 1927 *Stuff and Nonsense, and So On* collection. The full text can be found in: *The Complete Poems of Walter de la Mare* (London: Faber & Faber, 1969), pp. 874–5.

116 This is a reference to the first two chapters of *Alice in Wonderland*. In the first chapter, 'Down the Rabbit-Hole', Alice drinks from a bottle labelled 'DRINK ME'

and shrinks to a height of ten inches, with the words 'I must be shutting up like a telescope!' In the second chapter, 'The Pool of Tears', having consumed a cake labelled 'EAT ME', she grows to a height of more than nine feet, with the words, 'Now, I'm opening out like the largest telescope that ever was!'.

117 Grandville (Jean Ignace Isidore Gérard, 1803–47), French caricaturist and illustrator whose depictions of the world of animals had a considerable influence on E's own early drawings.

118 The word 'jelly' is in English in the original and presumably is meant to describe the quality of Disney's animation.

119 E was here speaking from his own experience during his visit to New York in 1930.

120 Lawrence's *St Mawr* was published in 1925. Ida Wylie, reviewing the novella for *Queen* (29 July 1925), p. 22, remarked: 'the splendid stallion which is the central figure is not merely an animal. It is the representative of freedom—of the power and beauty of life.' See: D. H. Lawrence, *St Mawr and Other Stories* (B. Finney ed.) (Cambridge: Cambridge University Press, 1983), p. *xxxviii*.

121 E's French is wrong here: it should read 'j'ai cité l'auteur', or 'I have cited the author.'

122 Agniya N. Kasatkina was an actress who studied with E under Meyerhold. She is said to have had a brief romance with E at the beginning of the rehearsals for *Enough Simplicity for Every Wise Man* in 1922.

123 Boris I. Arvatov (1896–1940) was an art historian and critic associated with the Proletkult and LEF. Vertoff

(written like this in E's original) is Dziga Vertov, the leader of the Cine-Eye group of documentary film-makers, with whom E often polemicized.

124 There is anecdotal evidence to suggest that Vertov was attracted to Kasatkina at the same time.

125 At this time the Herzen House in central Moscow was owned by the Union of Soviet Writers and partly inhabited by writers and others.

126 'Madame' was E's nickname for Elizaveta S. Telesheva (1892–1943), an actress and director at the Moscow Arts Theatre who played the chairperson of the kolkhoz in *Bezhin Meadow* [1935–37] and, according to some accounts, became E's 'civil' wife.

127 By 'national', E means a member of one of the Soviet Union's many national minorities.

128 Vera D. Yanukova (1904–39) played the role of Mamayeva in *Wise Man*, the reworking by Sergei M. Tretyakov of *Enough Simplicity for Every Wise Man*, the comedy by Alexander N. Ostrovsky (1823–86), which E directed for Proletkult in 1923. She was allegedly also emotionally involved with E.

129 Isidore Ducasse, Comte de Lautréamont (1846–70), French writer, whose major work was the collection of prose poems, 'Les Chants de Maldoror' (1869). He was later acknowledged as a precursor of Surrealism.

130 *Merbabies*: The Russian title is *Podvodnyi tsirk* [Underwater Circus].

131 E's reference.

132 Leo Tolstoy, 'Kholstomer' in *The Insiders and Other Stories*, VOL. 12, *The Novels and Other Works* (E. Hapgood trans.) (New York: Scribner's, 1913), pp.

240–1. The title has sometimes been translated as 'Strider'.

133 Caroline F. Spurgeon, *Shakespeare's Imagery and What It Tells Us* (Cambridge: Cambridge University Press, 1935).

134 E uses the English word 'tall' here. The Russian editors have translated this back into Russian as 'extravagant', which possibly makes more sense in this context.

135 Yvette Guilbert (1867–1944) was a French chanteuse and actress. E devoted a chapter of his memoirs to her: 'The Lady with the Black Gloves', *ESW4*, pp. 258–63; see also pp. 124–6.

DISNEY AND
OLD NORSE ART

Disney's film about mosquitoes.[1]

Mosquitoes swarm the whole time—and the swarm is like a common collective body. In the end they swarm into one black spot with a common contour, echoing that of a single small mosquito! I.e. into one large mosquito!!!

This has an exact *Vorstadie*[2] [prior stage] in Scheltema's *Altnordische Kunst* (p. 193: *ornamentale Tierscherze* [ornamental animal jokes].

This is repeated on the threshold of the Renaissance—in Dante's *Paradiso* the soudl so the rulers take the shape of an eagle.

In Japanese caricature. A large cat's head comprised of cats. A human head of humans, and so on.

Here the portrait of Commander-in-Chief Nikolai Nikolayevich, composed of the faces of German officers.[3]

The head of Satan, composed of women's bodies. Some American Job composed of minute bodies, etc.

The very urge is apparently the 'reconstruction' *der Zellenförmigkeit*—of the cellularity of a living organism *an der unteren Schwelle* [on the lower threshold] ... and of a soc[ial] organism *an der oberen* [on the upper] (a nation as a body and the tsar-leader as embodying the nation in himself—China).

Nations represented by a *single* person: England and John Bull, the USA and Uncle Sam (provide exhaustive information about 'Uncle Sam'—I had something somewhere from 'US Uncle Sam) ...

(It is interesting that nations are also totemic: the British lion, the French cockerel, the Russian bear.)

DISNEY (both for him as such and for the transition to Thurber-Steinberg.)[4]

Cité d'après [Cited after] *Cartoon Cavalcade*, edited by Thomas Craven, pages 247, 248:

Disney's drawings are created of and for the motion picture, and no reproduction of them in the form of still life can give more than a faint idea of their beauty and vitality when seen on the screen. Because he knows this better than anyone else, he does not judge his drawings by the commonly accepted standards of art.

He explained the difference to me in a few words. 'How does an artist paint a coat?', he asked. 'Well', he answered, 'that depends on the artist, of course. If he is a realist, he paints the texture of the cloth, shows how the folds of the cloth conform to the lines of the body, and maybe, if he is a stickler for details, he paints in the buttons. If he is a Cézanne, he makes the body solid. But, whatever kind of artist he may be, he gives you a piece of tailored cloth hung on the human frame. That's not the way we do it. We put a coat on a man and tell him to get going, and, as he walks, we watch for indications of motion. The cloth will wrinkle at the elbows and under the arms, and those wrinkles are the clues. We emphasize and repeat them from drawing to drawing, and wear the wrinkles together into a pattern to create fluidity and rhythm. Everything we do is directed towards one end—and that end is movement. That's how we draw a coat. And incidentally, we never draw elbows or joints—they interfere with the rhythm. Everything is in a state of flux with us.

The alpha and the omega of Disney's method.[5]

The return to a state of flux.

Even 'plasmatically' down to the details—avoiding even in the subject-matter the stage of ossification in the couplings—remaining a the stage of flow—fluctuation!

Thurber moves along the same lines (and Steinberg possibly even more so).

Here the style of the graphic (in the manner of the stroke and in the construction of the form) attempts to produce this very fluctuation (fluidity) through the static nature of drawing using its own methods: Thurber's plasmatically flowing figures.

But the fluidity of Thurber's forms crosses over into a fluidity of meanings.

(Transition: the fluidity of images, flowing into one another: 'House and Woman', p. 348, Carnaval [in the book] *Men, Women and Dogs*. N.B. Cf. the analogies in Werner's child's drawing.[6]

Merging the two themes together . . .

8 July 1946 [7]

Breathing, spirit, voice—these are symbols of potentiality (cf. Marie Bonaparte's analysis of Edgar Allan Poe's *Perte d'haleine* [*Loss of Breath*] as a story about the loss of potentiality).[8]

Hence, the image of omnipotence is extremely clear.

Moreover, the very hero is clearly phallic: the whale.

An omnipotent whale!

Cinema as extrapolated theatre.

And in this cinema, extrapolated theatre does make its appearance—not as filmed real theatre with real actors performing on the screen, but as drawn theatre.

(i.e. theatre that has twice been extrapolated—both in the field of technology and in terms of subject matter.)

And the phallus, the very one from the processions in whose honour theatre as such, legitimate theatre, was born, re-enters this trans-theatre [*za-teatr*].

By the way it re-enters literally: from the portal of the stage the whale enters into the auditorium. (N.B. The approach of the *Potemkin* and its guns directed at the auditorium.[9] Cf. one of the German theatres, following *Potemkin* in the same season, thrust the barrels of guns at the auditorium in a Bernard Shaw play. The same thing happened in *Roar, China!*[10]

The phallicity [*fallichnost'*] of the image of the Whale as *Urphallos* was exhaustively investigated by D. H. Lawrence with reference to *Moby Dick*[11] in *Studies in Classic American Literature.*

(Define more precisely the direct relationship between *Moby Dick* and Lewis Carroll's *The Hunting of the Snark*—perhaps there is an element of parody here? Or, is it simply a comic aspect of the same pursuit of potentiality that Melville resolves tragically?

A noter—Snark = Snake + Shark—[Carroll] furnishes [us with] such a labile image of the subject. Don't forget that Alice 'like a telescope' first grows, then gets shorter, and then her neck is stretched out!)

Here Disney is repeating the best traditions of American imagery!

In this respect the phenomenon of Willie's multiple voices [*mnogogolosost'*] is splendidly well read.

The *Urphallos* contains within it all the various individual personalities growing from a single root—male and female—and the many-voiced choruses of all living creatures!

The nature of these contents is emphasised once more by the secondary comic aspect of this same theme.

In the early stages of the development of humanity, being pregnant was inseparable from the notion of gorging oneself. Once upon a time people supposed that children are born from eating food. Gargantua is born after Mme Grandgousier ('Insatiable Gullet')—Gargamella— has gorged herself *d'un fort plat de tripes* [on a magnificent dish of tripe].[12] In *L'Assommoir*, Zola laughs at the pregnant Gervaise *qui a avalé un melon* [who has gorged a melon]. Let us not forget that early forms [of life] in the early stages of development—at the stage of the cell—do not yet distinguish between the twin processes of nutrition and reproduction.

The mediaeval conception of a spermatozoon was of a miniature person and it was thought that representatives of every future generation were immersed in one another (in a diminishing progression of examples), like the [seeds of the] rocket missile in Adam's sperm! (This was a graphically decorative, and therefore incorrect, image of what, in terms of structure and process actually does take place in a cellular organism.)

The whale-like phallus with its four and four hundred voices is even here represented in its correct preconscious field.

(See Blake's engraving of the stream of little humans in Laurence Binyon's book on English watercolours.)[13]

Word comes to the musical world of a singing whale. Tetti-Tatti, the great impresario of the Metropolitan, decides that Willie must have swallowed an opera singer. Having discovered great singers in fish markets, he hopes to find another star in a whale. He goes after Willie with a harpoon. When he finds him, Willie serenades Tatti with a trio from *Lucia*,[14] convincing Tetti that Willie is full of singers.

(N.B. 'swallowed'. 'full of'...)

But Disney also joins a traditional American figurative schema: that of Edgar Allan Poe, which is most keenly expressed in *The Pit and the Pendulum*.

Willie enters from the stage into the auditorium, in the same way that the pendulum enters the Inquisition prisoner's cell in this novella.

The mechanics of these ideas are unravelled by Marie Bonaparte in her two-volume psychoanalysis of Edgar Allan Poe.

These are *Mutterleibsversenkung*[15] + *Vaterleibseindringen* [Immersion into the mother's womb + Penetration of the father's flesh].

The act of fertilization, perceived inside out at the moment of completion.

There is something terrible in this (in Poe).

Here, the resolution is grotesquely comic.

An example of this kind of examination from inside is in 'Le visage vu de l'intérieur', an article in the journal *Verve*, nos 5–6 (1939), devoted to the human body.

The paradoxical nature of this way of posing the question and of this point of view is, as we see, entirely logical.

I also resolve this image in its tragic aspect in exactly the same way in *Ivan the Terrible*.

Moskvin[16] asks me what the general atmosphere should be for the scene where Vladimir is murdered. How should we comprehend the Cathedral for this scene.

I tell him through an image—'The Cathedral as a belly. Ivan enters it in the same way that the father penetrates the mother.'

In terms of colour and shot level that is precisely how I construct it.

Two walls of oprichniki make way and Ivan enters [through] this narrow passage.

Ivan in a skull-cap—conical-phallic [*konifallichen*].

A noter! By way of gossip, from the very first steps of my work Ivan has always figured in my caricatures in the shape of a phallus. Young and powerfully erect in his speech in the Uspensky Cathedral and on through various phases until he is limp and drooping in old age. Made a complete set of these drawings for Cherkasov and he has kept them. We call this 'working on the part'.[17]

The grotesque caricature quality (also overemphasised from the examples) means nothing as a form: nevertheless the phallic imagery is there.

From the position of Vladimir we have his return to the womb, the terrifying labyrinth of the Minotaur, *à l'envers* to the point of NOTHING: Vladimir is killed, he is reduced to zero.

The usual Son-Father (Oedipus) drama that runs through the major part of my work (Abraham and Isaac in *Bezhin Meadow*—that is why I probably chose it and got excited about the stuff).

My passion for *The Brothers Karamazov*,[18] which I wanted to film in 1942 (Alma-Ata), and so on.

••

The subject-matter of *Willie, The Hunting of the Snark* and *Moby Dick* is the same in its basic characteristic—the hunting and the attempt to capture the whale (the Sperm Whale, as the Americans and Melville call it throughout).

Lawrence interprets this subject as the recapturing of sexual potency.

In Carroll's personal drama this is very plausible. (You probably *tambien* [also].) In Disney it is not so much personal as located in relation (in a distorting mirror) to the contemporary world: Lawrence judges the America of the past through the America of today.

Lawrence's introductory thoughts are lampoon-like, identical to the caricatured interpretation of this subject matter in Disney.

The whale is killed by a harpoon and ascends to Heaven—de-sexualization, castration, etc these are essentially the same tragic theses of Lawrence presented here in comic aspect and comic only because they are basic.

In general terms, no less an indictment of America than Lawrence's writings.

And of course the image of Paradise is very beautifully achieved through the mortification of the flesh, ascesis and the castration of the phallic basis.

The whale's emergence on to dry land corresponds to evolutionary imagery.

It is interesting that the title of the article on *Willie* is 'Melodious Mammal Seen Again'.

From the unfinished material on the subject of *The Mystery of Evolution*.

P.S.

And, finally, as always:

Artur Aksyonov comes to Kratovo—by chance.[19]

With a bundle of newspapers and books that he has seized—by chance.

Amongst them is *Life* for 11 March 1946 (might it be the 4th or 18th??!)—by chance.

In precisely this issue there is something about *Willie* by chance.

How appropriate.

And how necessary!

NOTES

1 I have been unable to identify this film definitively, although it is not unknown for E's references to be mistaken, in which case this *may* be a reference to the short cartoon film, *The Mosquito* [USA, 1945], directed by Mannie Davis, not for the Disney studio, but for the rival Terrytoons series.

2 E mistakenly uses *Vorstadie* here instead of *Vorstadium*.

3 Grand Duke Nikolai Nikolayevich Romanov (1856–1929) was Commander-in-Chief of the Russian armies in 1914–15.

4 James Thurber (1894–1961) and Saul Steinberg (1914–99) were American humorists who both worked for *The New Yorker*. E's personal library contained copies of Thurber's *Men, Women and Dogs* (1943) and Steinberg's *All in Line* (1945).

5 E uses the word *sistema* [system], used in Russian to describe Stanislavsky's 'method'.

6 See p. 152, n. 91.

7 This is a continuation of the previously published note written at Kratovo on the same day. See pp. 148–52.

8 *Loss of Breath* was first published under that title in 1835.

9 A reference to the closing scene of E's *The Battleship Potemkin*, in which the battleship heads for the audience, appearing to tear the screen in two as it does so.

10 Presumably a reference to a production of Shaw's *Major Barbara. Roar, China* by Sergei M. Tretyakov (1892–1939), directed by Meyerhold, was premiered in Moscow in January 1926, exactly one year after *Potemkin* in a staging clearly influenced by E's film.

11 *Moby Dick* was a whaling adventure published in 1851 by the American writer Herman Melville (1819–91) and is considered by many to be the greatest work of American fiction. Chapter 11 of Lawrence's *Studies in Classic American Literature is* devoted to *Moby Dick* (London: Penguin, 1971), pp. 153–70. On p. 169 of that edition, Lawrence describes the dead whale as 'The last phallic being of the white man'. Chapter 6 of Lawrence's study is devoted to Edgar Allan Poe.

12 Reference to the novel *Gargantua and Pantagruel* by the French writer François Rabelais (1494–1553).

13 William Blake (1757–1827), English painter, poet and visionary. Laurence Binyon, Keeper of Prints and Drawings at the British Museum, published a number of works on this subject but it seems most likely that this reference is to *English Water-Colours* (London: A. & C. Black, 1933).

14 *Lucia di Lammermoor* (1835, revised 1839) was the tragic opera by Gaetano Donizetti (1797–1848) and based on Sir Walter Scott's novel *The Bride of Lammermoor*.

15 Cf. 'Monsieur, madame et bébé', *ESW4*, pp. 487–506.

16 Andrei N. Moskvin (1901–61) was E's cameraman for the interior scenes in this film.

17 Nikolai K. Cherkasov (1903–66) was the actor who played the title roles in both *Alexander Nevsky* and *Ivan the Terrible*.

18 Novel by Fyodor Dostoyevsky.

19 Artur Aksyonov worked for VOKS, the All-Union Society for Foreign Cultural Links, and was thus able to supply E with foreign newspapers and magazines such as the copy of *Life* mentioned here.

From Eisenstein's childhood drawings. 'In the World of Animals',
Riga, 1913–14. (Eisenstein Cabinet)

APPENDIX
[NOTES ON DRAWING]¹

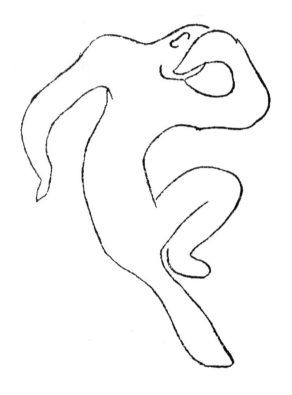

I

[Moscow], *14 September 1932*

Why are my drawings, despite a complete lack of anatomical feasibility, humanly physiologically disturbing for
viewers? Would it not seem that 'not anatomical' means
'not imitative'? The point is that these drawings are *proto-
plasmic, avant tout.* And elemental because they capture the
process between the primal protoplasm and formed man.

In my drawings, the truly appealing theme is *the coming
into being* of the human form from plasma (in this lies the
attractiveness of Olaf Gulbransson—cite his drawings).[2]

NOTES ON DRAWING · **179**

TOP: 'Another Salome'. Olaf Gulbransson (1914).
BOTTOM: 'Olaf Plays the Flute'. Self-caricature by Olaf Gulbransson (1914).

Mickey Mouse—the first factual dynamic drawing—has this plasmation par excellence:

here is the true basis of that which I reduced in Kretschmerian limits to plant vegetation (as a plant).

This is the plasmatizing of solid objects: the stretching of necks, legs, the rhythmical swaying of trees, of solid figures etc.

Note too the disintegration and assembling, very frequent in Disney, like quicksilver scattering and rolling back into a cohesive little ball.

It is curious that this plasmatic tradition is also found in comical *non-drawn* tricks:

the elastic steam engine from some old comedy, panting from the heat. Or the fight in a safe between a group of hunters and a lion where the safe becomes elastic (a balloon), and the movements of the whole fight are visible.

••

To this one can attribute in general the tradition of mutually penetrating objects in painting and drawing.

These too are plasmatic reminiscences: Picasso, Annenkov (especially), Grigoriev etc.[3]

TOP & FACING PAGE: Georges Annenkov, illustrations to Alexander Blok's
poem, *The Twelve* (1918)

FACING PAGE: Boris Grigoryev, 'Portrait of V. Meyerhold' (1922)
TOP: Untitled painting from Grigoryev's collection, *Rasiya* (1922)

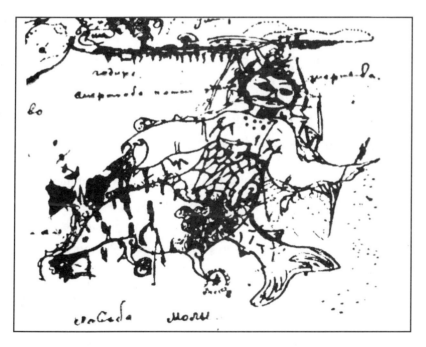

Velimir Khlebnikov, facsimile of manuscript drawing.

With them, this turns into the sticking of certain objects into others.

With the Surrealists: Dali, for example—even the very objects become plasmatic (for example, a drooping watch, folded over like a crêpe)...[4]

Revealing are the drawings of the full-blooded ecstatic—Khlebnikov[5]—being, in general, nothing more than the slightly personified fabric of plasma, fully resembling illustrations for a physiological atlas.

15 September 1932

Arms and legs in my drawings are always ... pseudopods of the primal plasma-amoeba.

21 September 1932

In drawings of the accompanying type (N.B.: very similar to the 'Macbeth' series)[6] there is yet another 'plasmatic' factor: the figures 'hover' in space; that is, the atavism in them belongs to the period before being set upon solid ground, to the amoebic-plasmatic stage of movement in liquid.

This is the graphic equivalent to the sensation of 'flight' among ecstatics: an identical uterine sensation of gyroscopicness and the identical phylogenetic pre-stage—the floating of the amoebic-proto-plasmatic state in a liquid environment.

'Samson and Delilah'. Undated drawing by Eisenstein.
(Eisenstein Cabinet)

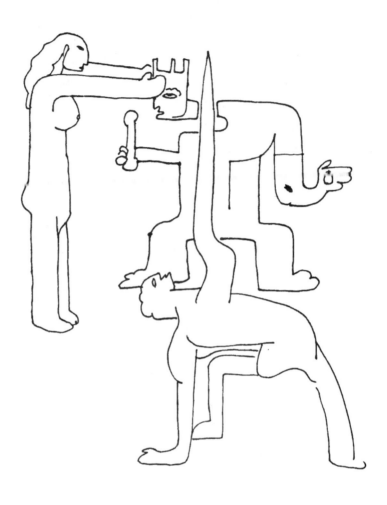

ABOVE AND FOLLOWING THREE PAGES: Eisenstein's 'Macbeth' series, c. May/June 1931. (Eisenstein Cabinet)

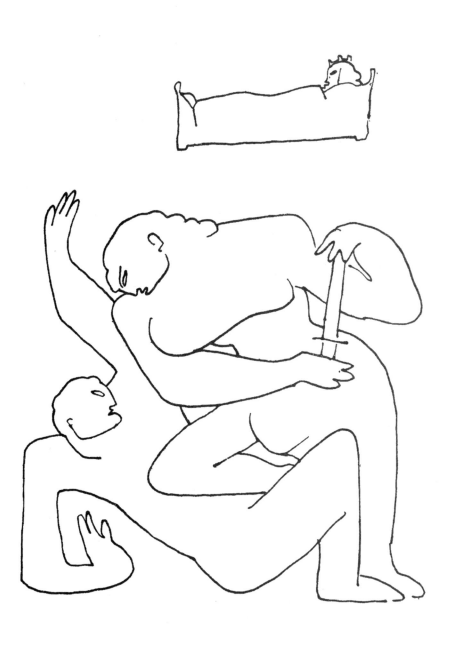

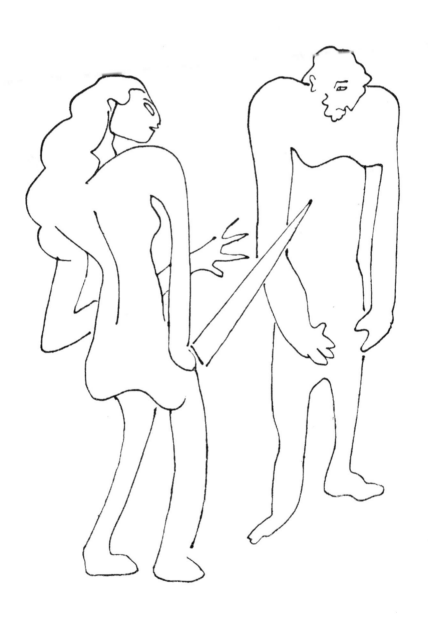

II

I am slightly troubled by one apparent controversy in my conception of the principle of composition.

Namely: the principle consists of the fact that a compositional formula is the content of what is represented, taken to the limits of generalization—the three or four strokes dividing the canvas and indicating the direction of the leading sections.

The unity of the representation and the thus-understood principle of composition also constructs that which we (I) call—an image, imagery. (For colour, its analogy is in the formula of the correlations of values.)

Each taken separately is incomplete and lacking imagery.

Representation alone is naturalism and 'itinerancy'.

Composition alone is Constructivism.

Nun aber kommt die Frage [Now, however, the question arises]: how does this fit into the general formula of the concept of art as a unity of the logical and the pre-logical, the sensuous?

In other words:

the 'logical' side—this, of course, is 'subject', 'anecdote', theme, content—that is, a narrowly understood representation (a horse, a bouquet, a flogging, a bankruptcy);

the pre-logical and sensuous component must comprise composition—and this par excellence, for it is the limit of maximal emphasis on form (even the conception of form).

It turns out, however, that composition is the (even highest) degree of generalization; that is, something which would seem to be the furthest removed from the sensuous and pre-logical—rather the abstract and super-logical!

The controversy is seeming, and results from a superficial understanding of the nature of . . . generalization, or rather from a lack of indoctrination in the problem of the nature of generalization, resulting from the purely colloquial use of this word.

Generalization is truly *super-logical*, but at the same time, unavoidably dialectical. And as such, it is also simultaneously (Lenin's as if) sub-logical.

That is, to external appearances, identical and alike, but in essence (nature) with a certain adjustment (by means of an intermediate link).

Is there a *similarity* between a pre-logical representation and a post-logical generalized representation?!

Of course!

Let us follow the crudest, plastic trait: in both, instead of a representation (objectively complete), there are *signifying strokes*—a 'pattern' (cf. the material on this in the German edition of Kretschmer's *Medizinische Psychologie*[7] —about schizophrenics and the abstraction of schematism).

The compositional skeleton of, say, Rubens' *Descent From the Cross*—the pattern of the arrangement of the figure—is absolutely identical in appearance to the cave-wall representation of man: the stick-figure devils or the little figures drawn by Indians on buffalo hides.

In both, there is a linear *pars pro toto*.

And the difference?

The difference is that the primal, sensuous *pars pro toto* takes any trait in place of the whole, while at the higher stage of *pars pro toto*, the generalization (a

Saul Steinberg, untitled drawing from *All in Line* (1945).

generalized image—in contrast to a real image, which unites a generalized image—composition—with an object: a representation) is the unique trait that completely embodies the principle of the whole (the most important thing about the whole).

The first stage is conventionally agreed upon—accessible by agreement to the initiated—the hieroglyphic-runic stage of a secret, conventional language.

The second is universally accessible, universally readable—preserving the primitivism of direct (sensuous) perception together with cognition, deliberately based upon the analysed essence.

III

ON A CERTAIN GRAPHIC EFFECT

12 October 1946

I have the habit of drawing on the blackboard a lot when I lecture.

I invariably draw my figures like this:

and I must say that they have an extraordinarily dynamic character. Sofia Kasyanovna Vishnevskaya,[8] at one of my lectures in 1939, pointed out that I always draw them with a closed contour.

Apparently, it is precisely from this that they obtain such a dynamically intense effect.

Where does this effect come from?

I think it is a threefold cause.

1. On a direct, objectively-representational basis.

What we really draw is the cryptogram which the spectator subconsciously reads as the most important, basically subconscious, really important and impressing part of the drawing.

This then develops into the 'imagery' of composition.

Here great, for it is completely basic—cellular, plasmatic: pseudopods.

2. On the basis of graphic dynamics, *als Auswuchs* [as an offshoot] of the fact that they are read as a pseudopod—that is, as a trace of movement.

3. On a physical basis in the representation—the tendency of a drop towards a circle (*also etwas* [therefore something] underlying even to the plasma).

A resulting drawing, therefore, is like a large, deliberate rebuff to this tendency.

4. Just as conflictive on the physical basis of *drawing conduct*.

The primal ellipse *im Kritzeln* [in scribbling] in children's pre-representational 'conduct' with a pencil, then extended to the object of representation (cf. the journal by Saudek).[9]

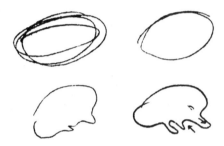

It is as if the ellipse pushes in and out, settling on the object according to its contour.

The drawings of Covarrubias (*Negro Drawings*).[10]

Remarkable!

Saul Steinberg[11]—whose drawings, in actuality, arose at first from a bent wire! (Written about somewhere in *Life*).

He even has a drawing where this is depicted! And this mark serves as an epigraph on his first album.

(N.B. cf. Cocteau's[12] waxed thread drawings and their imprint on his graphics.)

This very same thing is also present in three-dimensional figures: from which comes the amazing expressiveness (i.e. a plastic embodiment of conflicts!) in the plastics of clay figurines—Mexican clay primitives (cf. the collection of specimens from the collection on Diego Rivera,[13] or *Medieval American Art*).[14]

Our Vyatka toys[15] are the same, and this is one of the secrets of their irresistible appeal.

The tendency towards a sphere. Everything pushed out beyond the limits of sphericalness—like an *Aufgedunsenheit* [swelling] from within or a pressure from outside—that is, the interrelation and interplay of several conversely directed forces. And again, an *Ebenbild* [similarity] to pseudopods, forced out by an impulse from within and pushed back into a ball-sphere by the pressure of the ectoplasm (an external pressure, as opposed to the endoplasm).

Thurber's[16] drawings are interesting in that he half submits to the factual dynamics of the play of lines in a plane

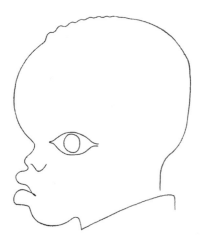

Miguel Covarrubias, *Negro Drawings* (1927)

TOP: James Thurber, untitled drawing from *Men, Women and Dogs* (1943).
BOTTOM: Tarascan clay figures, *c.* 15th century.

Untitled drawing by Eisenstein, dated 20 October 1946.

and half portrays the three-dimensional clay figures of the type of the Mexican primitives.

(A sensation of an illusory ballish roundedness accompanies Thurber's linear outlining.)

Volume in Steinberg is more planar—his closed surfaces appear as *schräggestellte* [slanted] planes—volume and space are constructed on the model of counter-reliefs.

But not like Thurber's.

The importance of all this analysis (here, of course in purest form—purer is not to be found) lies, of course, in he context of the thesis about the 'second plane' *jedes Gebietes* [of every realm] given by the basis on which the appearance stretches.

Cf. the primitivism of the *subtext*, that is, the true theme of a phrase. (Here belongs the Freudian slip) and the necessity of a 'complex' underlying the situation ('Oedipus' in *Hamlet*), etc.[17]

NOTES

1 This text is extracted from E's unpublished 'Work Notes'.

2 Olaf Gulbransson (1873–1958) was a Norwegian caricaturist and illustrator, popular for his satirical drawings in the German magazine *Simplicissimus*. His work exerted an undeniable influence on E's own graphic style.

3 Pablo Picasso (1881–1973), Spanish painter, sculptor and graphic artist.

   Yuri [Georges] P. Annenkov (1889–1974), Russian artist who lived in Paris from 1924. E met him in Paris in 1929/30, when Annenkov sketched his portrait.

   Boris D. Grigoriev (1886–1939), Russian painter, illustrator and caricaturist. Lived abroad after 1919.

4 Salvador Dalí (1904–89), Spanish painter, sculptor and graphic artist whose talent for self-publicity made him one of the most famous members of the Surrealist group. He described his pictures as 'hand-painted dream photographs'. One of the haunting images recurring in his paintings was that of the 'drooping

watch', which appeared for instance in 'The Persistence of Memory' [1931].

5 Velimir (Viktor K.) Khlebnikov (1885–1922), Russian poet associated with the Futurists who developed the notion of 'trans-sense' sounds.

6 E produced nine graphic series (more than 150 drawings) on the theme of 'The Murder of King Duncan' from Shakespeare's *Macbeth* in Mexico in May–June 1931.

7 Reference to: Ernst Kretschmer, 'Schizophrenic Thought Processes and Expressionism' in *Medizinische Psychologie* [Medical Psychology], 3rd EDN (Leipzig: G. Thieme, 1926). In E's copy the following confession by one of Kretschmer's patients is underlined: 'I visualize all outward forms in terms of geometrical stylization— as triangles, squares and circles—I seek to schematize everything, to divest everything of the actual reality!'

8 Sofia K. Vishnevskaya (1899–1962) was a Soviet art director on stage and screen and the wife of the writer Vsevolod V. Vishnevsky (1900–51), whose stage style was influenced by E's *Potemkin*.

9 Robert Saudek (1880–1935), British psychologist and expert on graphology and founding editor of the journal *Character and Personality*. E owned a copy of Saudek's basic work *The Psychology of Handwriting* (London: Allen & Unwin, 1925), which he dated 8 June 1933.

10 Miguel Covarrubias (1904–57), Mexican painter, book illustrator and ethnographer. E purchased his album: Miguel Covarrubias, *Negro Drawings* (New York: Alfred A. Knopf, 1927) in Hollywood on 21 September

1930. It is possible that this book, together with the impressions made on him by ancient Mexican plastics, the engravings of José Guadalupe Posada, the frescoes of Rivera, Orozco and Siqueiros, helped stimulate E to take up drawing again after an eight-year break from 1923 to 1930.

11 See above, P. 183, n. 4.

12 Jean Cocteau (1889–1963), French poet, essayist, artist, film-maker and playwright whom E met in Paris in 1930. See also *ESW4*, pp. 240–52.

13 Diego Rivera (1886–1957), Mexican painter and muralist much inspired by traditional folk motifs. E claimed that it was a meeting in Moscow with Rivera that had first stimulated his fascination with Mexico: *ESW4*, pp. 372 & 412.

14 Pál Kelemen, *Medieval American Art: A Survey in Two Volumes* (New York: Macmillan, 1943).

15 The reference is to traditional Russian clay figurines produced in the northern Russian city of Vyatka (in 1946 Kirov). E's fondness for these toys is evidence not only of his personal collection of them: he viewed folk-art plastics as one of the prototypes of a genuinely national style of Russian cartoon. E expressed this idea in an article entitled 'The Vyatka Pony' in his book *Colour*, in which he reproached Soviet animators of the period for their blind imitation of Disney: *IP3*, pp. 500–12.

16 James Thurber (see above, p.183, n. 4) was a frequent contributor to *The New Yorker*. E owned a copy of his collection: James Thurber, *Men, Women and Dogs* (New York: Harcourt, 1943), which is dated 2 January 1946.

17 (Leyda's note) This last sentence reveals E's sarcastic atti-
tude towards the claims of the psychoanalytical school to
a universal explanation of art. Thus he rejected not only
the attempts of the Freudians to exhaust the plot conflict
of *Hamlet* with the aid of an 'Oedipus complex', but also
their tendency in general to reduce any artistic phenomenon to a set of psychological 'complexes' and 'traumas'. To
an equal degree E reacted in hostile fashion to the term
'subtext', seeing in it an analogy to the 'repression in the
subconscious' (according to Freud) of the true motif, which
'breaks out' in slips of the tongue, slips of the pen, unin-
tentional actions, inadequate intonations etc. In E's aesthetic system the point is not a 'non-coincidence of text
and subtext' but the essential dialectical contradiction
which determines the multiple levels of situations and the
multiple significance of artistic imagery.